Mystics:
A Thousand Paths To
A Single Door

by
Joseph Lumpkin

Mystics:
A Thousand Paths to a Single Door

First time or interested authors, contact Fifth Estate Publishers, Blountsville, AL 35031.

First Printing 2015

Cover Design by An Quigley

Printed on acid-free paper

Library of Congress Control No: 2015948118

ISBN: 9781936533596

Fifth Estate 2015

Dedicated to my grandfather, Rev. W. R. Lumpkin.
(1902-1988)
You were a potter who molded a thousand vessels.
Everyday I find your fingerprints on my soul.

Table of Contents

Introduction

To experience infinite love; To be one with the beloved; To know the eternal self; To feel time stand still; To live in the infinite now; To experience existence instead of simply existing; To merge with the all; To become nothing; To become everything; To encounter the real and timeless self; To feel heaven stand up; To be aware of the sublime; To become sublimely aware; To be filled with light; To have an unbearable sense of lightness; To be a wave on the infinite sea; To stop the mind and be completely still; To have a sense of unity; To be free of guilt and shame; To finally be at peace...

The mystical experience is an encounter with the true and ultimate reality in which there is a sense of sacredness so rich and beautiful it cannot be adequately described. The mystical experience is enlightenment, awareness, wakefulness, love, peace, and a million things more. It is nothing at all. It is the all. The experience may last but a moment but it can change your life.

It is available to all people in every breath of life. Some will stroll into it with ease. Some will grow slowly into a state of mystical maturity. Others will meditate for many years to be enlightened in the blink of an eye.

Some may reach the mystical experience of unity with god through service, others will awaken in meditation, study, nature, humanity, or even the dance of the Dervish, but no matter the path, all will enter the same gate.

What is mysticism, and what is this life-changing experience?

Mysticism (mys ti cism) is defined as the belief that union with or absorption into the Deity, the absolute, or the spiritual apprehension of knowledge inaccessible to the intellect, may be attained through contemplation and self-surrender.

It is important to note that the intellect or mind cannot apprehend the mystical state, and thus can become one of the greatest deterrents as the mind chatters and argues against its own stillness.

According to "Body, Soul and Spirit: The Mystical Experience Registry":
Mysticism is usually defined in dictionaries and encyclopedias as a spiritual discipline used to make contact with the divine. While this definition is frequently correct, there have been many people who have had mystical experiences without following a special discipline. Conversely, many people have followed a set of spiritual practices carefully and for a prolonged period but have never contacted the divine.

The mystical experience takes us beyond faith and religion. But the journey is not an easy one. It takes heart-wrenching emptiness to be filled with the "infinite now".

Interior experiences, those that are spiritual or mystical in nature, lack common language. There are no tangible points of reference neither in direction nor place that we may compare and establish mutual terms. It is because of this lack of spiritual language that the mystical experience cannot be easily explained. It is alluded to, pointed at, and explained by allegory and metaphor at best.

The mystical experience transcends religion, sect, denomination, and faith. It goes beyond any personal idea of who or what God may be. Faith in God, Elohim, Allah, Jesus, or the Buddhist concept of emptiness and detachment can all yield the mystical experience. Indeed, even those who have no fixed idea of God or any belief at all have reported mystical experiences. For each person that has an experience there will be a different description. In this state, God is both male and female. God is the lover and beloved.

Each path is different and each leads to a mystical journey, which is so similar that the mystics of these various systems share a common experience.

Some paths are easier than others for the Western mind to understand. Mystics in the Christian and Muslim traditions usually begin their journey within a religious framework, and then transcend religion all together, by experiencing unity with the source of love itself. Some seekers focus on one thing. Others clear their mind of everything. Those focusing on a single thought explain the feeling that their entire world is brought to a laser point of thought, and then the point disappears, leaving them in nothingness.

Indeed, Christian mystics of the Middle Ages taught that any creature, creation, idea, or thought is not God. Thus to remove all creatures, creations, ideas and thoughts would leave only God. This process is called, "The Cloud of Unknowing."

Secular mystics encounter the divine state of humanity. Martial artists may obtain the mystical state through meditation and "one point concentration" within each technique. Zen practitioners clear their mind to achieve "no-mindness" in order to see the truth of existence without the distortion of ego. Meditation can take many forms. The usual mode that comes to mind is sitting quietly and calming the mind. But meditation can be active, such as martial arts or yoga. Meditation may be all but invisible and consists of a thought or idea placed in the back of the mind so it subconsciously boils until revelation bubbles up from deep within.

Mystics feel, know, and see the connection between all sentient beings and thus gain reverence for each person and every living thing. This living energy or entity within each person is seen as separate from the body carrying the divinely given life. Life, they say is older than anything living. One of the most important and oft repeated themes of insight during the state of altered reality is the realization that we are not our bodies. The mystic may find themselves outside the body, floating above, watching the scene play out. The observer is the real and eternal self.

At times this kind of "detachment with love" is carried forward from the experience. The mystic becomes the observer. Becoming the observer means being aware of our real self, separate from ego, fear, or desire so we are capable of observing how we are reacting. We have a level of self-awareness so we do not get caught up in a situation because we have gained the ability to objectively observe what is transpiring.

Although the observer is part of the process and carries an intimate knowledge of what is being observed, the observer is an objective witness, knowing that what is happening will not affect their eternal self. The observer can attest to the truth of what occurred without the details being colored by ego, pride, desire, or fear. More importantly, all this is done with an effectual compassion, which comes from spiritual contact with the author of life.

The most heart wrenching transformation is seeing the truth of one's deeds, thoughts, and behavior in the raw light of objective truth. It will pierce the heart and bring the strongest man to his knees sobbing. Yet, at the same instant we are bathed in love, truth, and compassion.

There is a deeper and more meaningful step beyond the observer. Some refer to this as being "the witness." Although terms and definitions may vary between teachers or schools, the witness is both observing and involved in all aspects of life. They have the perspective of unity among all parties. We are one. The beloved and I are the same and all beings are one and equal because we are within the beloved and the beloved is within us. This is the state some refer to as "I and Thou".

Living life as the masses live, there is the perception of separation between others and us. We have our opinions and goals, which are more important than those of others. However, when we view ourselves as truly equal to others we have entered a state of love that is mystical. These states of being will be discussed further as we look into the deeper points of mysticism.

The mystical experience is personal and varies between each seeker but within the experience there are always commonalities. There is always a feeling of being touched by some higher and greater truth or power. Although there is no set pattern, in that one may proceed directly from the first question to complete enlightenment in a single step, there are stages that many follow.

One realizes there is a path and enters the stream.
One reaches a place of enlightenment but it quickly passes.
One has the ability to return to the state of bliss and may stay longer.
One abides in the place of enlightenment.

The energies of love, compassion, and enlightenment follow the same rules of any energy in the universe. It can flow through us. It can be reflected by us. It can be absorbed and re-emitted from us. The energy is never lost. This is the same law of thermal-dynamics in the physical world. It is written, "As above, so below," and the mystic experiences this same law from a "higher power."

These experiences may occur inside or outside of a religious tradition or practice. Some religions embrace the mystical experience as a sign of spiritual growth. Because one is encountering the divine, the mystical experience allows us to glimpse for a moment the interconnected all and thus it engenders a moral and ethical sense. Yet, because the mystical experience links the person directly to the source, exclusive of religious trappings, structure, or control many religions have sought to stifle the mystical element. Throughout history religious establishments have actually persecuted and killed mystics, even those of their own belief. In spite of this, no religion or outside force can halt the internal journey. From the time humans looked up to heaven, seekers have walked this sacred path, and the results have kept the light burning in a dark world.

Mystics have been known by various names. Terms such as shaman, wise man, monk, ascetic, seeker, transcendental, guru, swami, yogi, prophet, priest, and visionary have been used to label those who view the spirit world differently than the rest. All describe the beauty of the experience.

The most beautiful and profound emotion we can experience is the sensation of the mystical. He to whom this emotion is a stranger, who can no longer wonder and stand rapt in awe, is as good as dead. To know that what is impenetrable to us really exists, manifesting itself as the highest wisdom and the most radiant beauty, which our dull faculties can comprehend only in their primitive forms - this knowledge, this feeling, is at the center of true religion. - Albert Einstein

The external enemy of mysticism is anything that keeps the focus on physical properties or interference, such as rules, doctrine, restrictions, ceremony, control through power structures, oversight, peer pressure, and strict religious form. These keep us from the interior journey. It is not that we must renounce religion but it cannot constrain us from our personal spiritual journey. The mystic must shake lose constraints, which keep the seeker from walking the path of awakening.

The internal enemies of mysticism are those things in ourselves, which would keep us from seeing the universal nature of humanity and the eternal nature of the spirit, both the universal divine spirit and our own spirit in service to the former as it (he/she, for the spirit has no gender and is all shades of gender within itself) is expressed through us.

Self-righteousness
Self-centeredness
Self-will
Self-importance
Desire
Passion
Greed

Or, as the Bible lists the issues in 1 John 2:15:
Do not love the world nor the things in the world. If anyone loves the world, the love of the Father is not in him. 16For all that is in the world, the lust of the flesh and the lust of the eyes and the boastful pride of life, is not from the Father, but is from the world.

But how do we embrace the journey and avoid the pitfalls? There are many paths that can take us in our desired direction. Most major religions have their mystics. Each presents a path of its own, and all are similar.

One driving force in all mystics is a heart that burns for the beloved. What is a mystic but someone chasing the divine flame? But if the fire is not hot and pure the smoke will blind us. Because the mystical experience occurs in many different and varying religions, and outside of religion, we will take a look at the journey and the result of the mystical journeys within some of our major faiths, and also in the non-religious or secular world. By examining such manifold viewpoints and explanations the depth and breadth of the mystical encounter may be better understood and help us along our journey to the heart of the divine.

It is hoped that the meager work before you may open to you avenues and thoughts that may lead you to a deeper life. Each chapter will begin with a religion or system that has yielded in the past great mystics. The religion or system will be examined. Following the brief identification of the approach there will be quotes, thoughts, and observations directly from the mystics themselves. In this way insights into their path and state of mind and spirit can be seen and felt.

Religion:
The Spiritual Awakening

Religion can be broadly understood as a system of beliefs and practices concerned with sacred things and/or symbols uniting individuals into a single moral community. The religious laws, rituals, and beliefs form a cohesive moral structure. If "religions" are not specifically related to the sacred, one could use the same definition for governments. Religions can and have become governments unto themselves. Therefore, a "religion" does not require a supernatural being as the object of worship, but it does have to represent a commitment to a particular moral or ethical code. An example is Buddhism, which claims no particular idea of god but is still considered a religion.

In the pre-Axial Age, religion always revolved around a deity. After the Axial Age, some religions, such as Buddhism, did not revolve around a god, but involved an inward journey toward deeper self-awareness.

In "The Great Transformation," Karen Armstrong plunges into the thick of history's confusion, injustice and conflict that have been humankind's companion as far back as we can reliably trace. In the period between 900 and 200 BCE, which she calls the Axial Age (a term borrowed from the German philosopher Karl Jaspers) — "humanity" as we conceive of it "came into being," thanks to the insights elaborated in several extremely diverse yet complementary traditions: biblical monotheism, Greek rationalism, Hinduism, Buddhism, Confucianism and Taoism. "All the traditions that were developed during the Axial Age," Armstrong writes, "pushed forward the frontiers of human consciousness and discovered a transcendent dimension in the core of their being" — until dark forces pushed it aside.

Armstrong further suggests that the history of the last two and a half millennia is seen as a continuous struggle between those who acknowledge and value the newly evolved spiritual insights and those who may have a much older and more restrictive concept of the nature of religion.

There is no way to know the number of mystics or progressive religious thinkers that influenced changes in the ancient world's religions, but archeology shows us that changes were molded mostly, if not totally, by migrations to and from adjacent regions, mixing cultures and gods.

This does not answer the nagging questions of why we persist in "structured" religions, and why all major religions carry the same moral or ethical imperatives. Jesus, among others, so beautifully summed up these imperatives: "Love God and treat others as you want to be treated." The rest is commentary.

Immanuel Kant (1724–1804) was a German philosopher who sought to find and identify the foundational principle of the metaphysics of morals. He attempted to analyze and articulate commonsense ideas about morality. Kant looked for the principles on which we base all of our ordinary moral judgments. He took the position that all rational people are born with an innate sense of morality. Thus, normal, sane, adult human beings will usually make the same judgment calls based on an inborn sense of right and wrong.

This is a wonderful idea, but seems rather naïve considering the amount of crime and abuse we see today. However, Kant could be correct but society and personal history may, as the Bible says, sear the conscience as with a hot iron. Neither does it answer certain questions such as, "If man is intrinsically good, why did we insist on human sacrifice in our past?" Today, crime runs rampant and Kant's theory does not seem to hold water. Possibly Kant's arguments only come to light when there are few negative social pressures involved. Studies have shown that the number of human sacrifices in primitive cultures rises rapidly under pressures of famine and pestilence. Under extreme circumstances, they sometimes turned to cannibalism.

There are at least two "wired in" processes going on here. The highest and oldest is self-preservation. The secondary impulse, which Kant describes, is based on following a social norm in order to enable the group, family, or tribe to survive. In other words, we are inclined to work as a team. This may explain our ability to stand by and see humans killed or sacrificed as long as the group acts in accord. We can call this a "mob mentality."

Perhaps there is something to this idea of humans drawing on some very widely shared moral viewpoint that contains some general judgments. Outside of the religious ceremony for punishing someone who has broken a moral imperative, such as – do not murder, do not steal – most societies do have the same basic moral structure.

Kant sought to discover a rational basis for the human sense of duty, and the principles by which one can distinguish between right from wrong. Right or wrong hinge on intent. The intention or motive for the action determines whether it is right or wrong. It opposes the view that the end justifies the means and does not account for the outcome of an action. In other words, modern society cares if death results from war, murder, self-defense, or accident.

Kant's starting point was his observation that we all experience an innate moral duty. Conscience triggers feelings of shame and guilt when we violate our internal moral compass. In this way, morality stands an empirical test. Since we seek to avoid the negative feelings of a remorseful conscience, we first attempt to do good. The highest form of good is "good will." To have good will, one must perform one's duty for the sake of duty and for no other reason.

From this, Kant concluded that moral duty is objectively revealed through reason. Morality can be known by using reason and can be verified or falsified.
To quote Kant:
"To act morally is to perform one's duty, and one's duty is to obey the innate moral laws."
"A good will is not good because of what it affects or accomplishes... it is good through its willing – that is good in itself."

If only a small seed of Kant's ideas are correct, it could answer the question of why religions in every corner of the globe have the same basic moral laws. Moral laws, however, are separate from religion. Religion is simply a vehicle for a moral code, since both religion and its commandments developed around the need to solidify and guide a society. Primitive man did not have courts. They had priests acting as judges.

So, why did this moral compass develop in humans? Possibly, it was due to a consequence of evolutionary pressures. Humans were weak, slow, hairless creatures in a world of beasts and natural elements. The only way to survive was to ban together. If a person went against the family, tribe, or group, he or she would be ostracized and would have to face the world alone. Loners did not survive well. Over time, those with the highest social quotient or teamwork flourished in the hostile environment. The good of the many won out over the good of the individual. This could be the beginning of our internal moral code. This code is at odds with the older code of individual survival. The greater imperative is personal survival at all cost. This impulse must be consciously overridden by communal cooperation. Herein is the difference between what Kant describes and what we see in society. Some people are balanced one way and some another.

This code is wired into our developing brains on a subconscious level. Meaning, the code could not be subjective since we had no way to "think" about it. However, it was made objective through the development of codified laws. Later, we grew and developed enough to intensely consider our laws, our conscience, and the internal battles.

Until the Axial Age, the focus of religion was external, particularly on rituals, laws, and ceremony intended to influence or control a god or gods to protect the family or tribe, bring rain, guarantee success in battle, and so on.

During the Axial Age, this changed and an internal search for god began. There may have been several influences driving this evolution. The world became smaller with migrations and the advent of transportation via horseback. Cities grew and developed, continuous warfare mixed gods as the conquered tribe adopted the beliefs of the victor, considering their gods as more powerful. The amalgam of tribes and formation of armies began the demise of tribalism and the splitting of families through death and conscription into military service. The shattering of tribes and families brought about the rise of individual focus. Previously, consequences or punishment from actions of one individual or tribal member affected the entire family or tribe. With individuals separated from families and tribes, the perpetrator carried the consequences alone.

Continual hardships of war, disease, and changes in societies caused people to question the efficacy of their traditional god and religious practices prompting them to look for alternatives.

In China, India, Greece, and Israel, the spirit of humankind awakened in a flash. Wise men, shamans, sages, prophets, philosophers, and scholars independently articulated their insights. The religious traditions they created or influenced are alive in the major religions of today. Confucianism, Taoism, Hinduism, Buddhism, philosophical rationalism, and monotheism arose as though they were orchestrated and coordinated by a single hand. The mystical consciousness, dormant in mankind burst forth like lightening.

The insights common to all religious enlightenment of the Axial Age include the ideas of reciprocity, compassion, love, altruism, and the individual's mandate to alleviate the suffering of others. The ideas of compassion and reciprocity are summed up in the actions of treating others justly and as you wish to be treated. Judaism would go on to embody these values in their laws. In turn, the newly awakened Judaism translated that ideal, which has evolved into a monotheistic religion in which members seek communion with God.

In the years centering around 500 BCE, great advances in religion, philosophy, science, democracy, and many forms of art occurred independently and almost simultaneously. Today, humanity still uses the spiritual foundations laid in that ancient time. In those times of social upheaval and political turmoil, spiritual and religious pioneers became the standard-bearers of a new religious, cultural, and social order. However, then as now, eighty percent of all religious pioneers will die in the wilderness, killed by those they were trying to lead to freedom. Great religious leaders rose up in various areas of the world attracting many followers, thereby changing many sociological, cultural, economic and spiritual beliefs.

In China, many individual thinkers, such as Confucius, Lao-Tse, and Mo Tzu, began to reflect on the ethical and spiritual implications of human existence. In time, their teachings became known throughout the world. Confucianism, Taoism, and Jainism are only a few religions to be founded or influenced by them.

In India, the authors of the Upanishads expanded the scope of their explorations to include metaphysical thinking in the search for the ultimate truth and the meaning of life and death.

India experienced a dramatic social and intellectual transformation, and produced the teachings of the Buddha and Mahavira. Like China, new teachings ran the whole gamut of philosophical schools of thought, including skepticism, materialism, and nihilism.

In Palestine, the prophets Elijah, Isaiah, and Jeremiah made their appearance. Although the law and moral code of the Israelites dates back before this age, and may have been influenced by the code of Hammurabi of 1750 BCE, the prophets reached beyond the law and called believers into a relationship with Yahweh.

This leap became the source of major and lasting cultural traditions enduring to the present time, giving way to a secondary stage or influence of spiritual transformation in which religions such as Judaism spawned the world's two major religions of Christianity and Islam.

In Greece, developments were more philosophical than spiritual. Greece witnessed the appearance of Thales, Xenophanes, and Heraclitus who regarded all existence to be in a state of flux, exemplifying his concept by stating, "one cannot step in the same river twice." Parmenides commented on the nature of permanent "being" as opposed to the impermanent phase of "becoming". Democritus devised the first atomic theory of nature, which later gave way to the scientific nature of matter and atoms.

These philosophers influenced the minds of Socrates, Plato, and Aristotle. They examined the very nature of existence, life, and thought, itself.

Each philosopher and thinker forced his or her culture to question and reinterpret previously devised cosmologies as they sought to bring reason into religion.

Even as philosophers were dividing science from religion, mystics were emerging from crystallized religions of old to seek the real internal world that lay beyond the senses. Some religions were born of pure spiritual and altruistic purpose. Others were born of selfish motives. Then, as now, many had their own agenda and pushed their own motives, calling it religion, and selling it to others.

Buddhism propagated the preaching of the eight-fold path. Right View and Right Intention are the wisdom factors of the Noble Eightfold Path. Right Speech, Right Action, and Right Livelihood address ethical conduct. Right Effort, Right Meditation, Right Concentration address mental cultivation. The wisdom factors of Right View and Right Intention are the foundation of all the other attributes.

The almost simultaneous changes in China, India, Palestine, and Greece seem too remarkable to be accidental; especially considering the lack of direct influence one movement could have had on another, considering the countries are widely separated from each other. The only example of intellectual communication among these countries appears to be the conjecture that in the 6th century BCE the Greek poet Alcaeus may have known the prophecies of Isaiah.

Slowly, religions began to influence and build on each other within different countries and cultures. Some religions became devoted to peace and the value all life. Others stalled in their warlike state. Ideas and beliefs of Jainism influenced a newly developing Hinduism and the new religion of Buddhism. The dualistic idea of good and evil contained within Zoroastrianism would influence the Jewish ideas of good and evil and the celestial war over man's soul. The new face of Judaism would give way to dualism in Christianity and Islam.

The idea of an "Axial Age" has no specific timeline. It is a general idea based around a broad period of time wherein a global awakening occurred, and religion once steeped in outward ritual turned inward and the idea of pleasing the gods turned into a search for god in us. This spiritual awakening within Judaism was the foundation that took the religion into a search for communion with God, as Abraham, the patriarch, followed by one prophet after another would forge the mystical path.

(Genesis 5:22-24) And after he became the father of Methuselah, Enoch walked with God 300 years and had other sons and daughters. {23} Altogether, Enoch lived 365 years. {24} Enoch walked with God; then he was no more, because God took him away.

(Genesis 6:8-9) But Noah found favor in the eyes of the LORD. {9} This is the account of Noah. Noah was a righteous man, blameless among the people of his time, and he walked with God.

(Exodus 33:11-17) The LORD would speak to Moses face to face, as a man speaks with his friend.

(James 2:23) And the scripture was fulfilled that says, Abraham believed God, and it was credited to him as righteousness, and he was called God's friend.

Thus the foundation was set for Christianity and Islam to build upon an ancient mystical path.

Jaspers' concept of the Axial Age is an observation and not a law of history. Yet, there were mighty spiritual changes taking place within the "Axial Age."

We will be examining some religions and paths established in and after the spiritual awakening of the Axial Age. We will see there are common foundational spiritual processes between all religions that produce mystics. All meditate. All do service for others. All seek to reach a state of stillness and focus of mind, which may allow the practitioners to an altered consciousness allowing them to transcend the ego boundary that separates us from the rest of the universe. Although there may be different paths the resulting mystical experience is the same.

Keep in mind the basic timeline of religious development – Hinduism 800-300BCE (based on the time the 11 major Upanishads were written including the ideas of reincarnation and karma - Buddhism 500BCE – Christianity 33 AD (Protestantism 16th century CE - Islam 622CE (Sufism 700CE).

We will examine the Christian mystics first, not because there is a preference, but because most readers will be familiar with the Christian faith. All mystics follow the same basic path and it would be easier to cover the common ground from the perspective of a known starting point.

Afterwards, we will examine the words and wisdom of mystics from various religions, cultures, as well as mystics from no religious background. As we examine various religions and paths it is not necessary that the reader believe or be a follower of that religion in order to glean the great wisdom offered by the mystic of its path. The light will shine through the covering of religion.

Christian Mystics

Christianity is a Middle Eastern religion. Christianity is an Abrahamic monotheistic religion based on the life and teachings of Jesus Christ as presented in the New Testament. It is the world's largest religion, with about 2.4 billion adherents, known as Christians.

Christianity began as a Second Temple Judaic sect in the mid-1st century.

The religion emerged in the Levant, and specifically in Judea. Levant is an approximate historical geographical term referring to a large area in the eastern Mediterranean. In its widest historical sense, the Levant included all of the eastern Mediterranean with its islands. It included all of the countries along the eastern Mediterranean shores, extending from Greece to Cyrenaica.

The term Levant entered English in the late 15th century to broadly refer to the eastern Mediterranean, including Greece, Anatolia, Syria-Palestine, and Egypt, that is, the lands east of Venice. Eventually the term was restricted to the Muslim countries of Syria-Palestine and Egypt.

Christianity spread initially from Jerusalem throughout the Near East, into places such as Aram (present day Syria), Assyria, Mesopotamia, Phoenicia, Asia Minor, Jordan and Egypt. In the 4th century it was successively adopted as the state religion by Armenia in 301 CE, Georgia in 319 CE, the Aksumite Empire in 325 CE, and the Roman Empire in 380 CE

After the Council of Ephesus in 431 CE the Nestorian Schism created the Church of the East. The Council of Chalcedon in 451

CE further divided Christianity into Oriental Orthodoxy and Chalcedonian Christianity. Chalcedonian Christianity divided into the Roman Catholic Church and Eastern Orthodox Church in the Great Schism of 1054 CE. The Protestant Reformation created new Christian communities that separated from the Roman Catholic Church and have evolved into many different denominations. Following the Age of Discovery, Christianity spread to the Americas, Australia, sub-Saharan Africa, and the rest of the world through missionary work and colonization. Christianity has played a prominent role in the shaping of Western civilization

Most modern Christians believe that Jesus is the Son of God, the messiah or anointed messenger. In the time of his teaching most people viewed him as a wise and enlightened man, having access to the heavenly realm. His teachings would have brought man into the right relationship with God and one another. Jesus was a mystic whose teaching of unity with the Father, forgiveness, peace, and love was so controversial that it led to his murder.

When Christianity first developed it was considered a sect of Judaism. Soon after the development of the sect the religion morphed from being the religion Jesus practiced to the religion based on Jesus.

In the following section we will see Christianity through the eyes of its mystics, those who were able to transcend doctrine and denomination to reach the heart of God.

TO KNOW HIM

Much of the spiritual life in Christianity has become superficial and narcissistic, a diluted pseudo Christianity mixed with Eastern occultism, so bogged down in doctrine and church laws as to be legalistic by nature and spiritually weak. It is possible the demise of contemplative worship is a direct result of an ever-accelerating lifestyle. We now live in a world where there are more and more people who live in greater and greater personal isolation, or possibly the better word is insulation. We interact as if we have a thickening armor over our hearts. We develop a skin to emotionally protect ourselves. The "skin" keeps the indignities forced on us by our society and our fellow man from harming us as much, but it is affecting our spiritual lives.

In the Christian church of today there is lack of commitment. We want to get to the conclusion before we get through the starting gate. Our fast-food religion focuses on one or two exciting and entertaining hours a week. There are no more voices crying in the wilderness because the wilderness of our hearts is left unexplored and there are none who dare venture into the dark regions of the soul. God waits for us in the quiet wilderness of our hearts. What shall we do?

The future of Christianity may lie solely in the mystical tradition, which demands a direct and personal relationship with God. Any hope of true salvation and personal growth in Christianity hinges on the depth of our relationship with Christ and his teachings. The entire Christian faith is supposed to be based on a direct and unique connection between the individual and God. In this aspect, Christianity is a mystical and dynamic faith. True Christian faith calls for union and communion with the Creator wherein He teaches us, guides us, and loves us.

Through meditation, adoration, and prayer we are joined with Him and transformed from within.

With most people, and sadly, with most Christians, a crucial gap remains between God and man. What is needed is not the teaching of doctrine, law, or church tradition, nor is it any social or moral message. We need a heart-to-heart dialogue with God.

Only when we realize we need and long for a relationship with our Creator in which He loves and teaches us as a father would a child will we begin to seek communion to "know" God. From the beginning He has bid us come, but the modern church has forgotten the path. It is still there, beneath the hedges of religion, pride, and tradition but the hedges must be cleared away to find the path.

One may think in reading this work it is a treatise against doctrine or opposed to theology. One may think it is purely a work calling us back to some simplistic, emotional, or childish view of faith. This could not be further from the truth. This is a call for balance, and a summoning of us inward and away from the superficial, outward-looking worship of today, away from the world. No matter the religion, rituals, rules, and exclusivity leads to a harsh and judgmental path.

This path is not simplistic, but it is simple. It is not childish, but it is childlike. It is not emotional but it gives way to a path, which leads to a depth beyond empty knowledge and passing emotion. This path will lead us to the heart of knowing. There we will see faith has been waiting all the while.

The formula of the worship of today is equal parts emotional gratification, superficial study of scripture, and adherence to rules of denomination. We have neglected the one thing that stands as the banner of Christianity - a relationship with God.

In the Christian narrative God seeks out man. God seeks to engage man in a relationship that is emotional and unique.

He extends his hand to us so we may see that He understands us. God demonstrated this by living as we live, suffering as we suffer, and experiencing life as only man can in order that He, God, might show us his compassion (a word meaning to suffer together) and empathy (meaning to feel the same thing) with us so that we may know He knows us and we may have a personal relationship with Him. For, if God is omniscient He would have already known what it was like to be man, but we could not have conceived of His knowledge.

In the story of Christ we see the hero-God-king who relinquished everything including His life in order to seek, love, and save his people. There is nothing left emotionally undone in this formula God has given us. It is in the church of today the formula becomes incorrect. Denominationalism has supplanted Scripture and following a set of rules has become more important than knowing He who made them. It is most essential to seek and know God, and to love Him, if we are to be changed by His love into His image. Only in this marvelous transformation can we hope to come close to doing what He has asked: Love God with your whole being. Love your fellow man as yourself.

But the study of theology does not serve to edify man. It seems almost arrogant to endeavor to study He who is omnipotent and omniscient. Learning scripture and points of doctrine serves to enhance our knowledge, but not our heart. We seek to gain insight into God's patterns and personality through study. This is admirable to a point; however, time may be best served by being in His presence. To know Him is always better than to study Him. To know Him is the mystical experience and the path followed by mystics of all faiths.

A GIFT OF LOVE

Mysticism – The doctrine that communion with God and a knowledge of the divine essence may be attained independent of the senses or processes of reason through intuition and insight; hence, the ecstasy of those who claim they have had insight or vision bringing them into spiritual union with the eternal and giving them knowledge of the supernatural. Webster's New School & Office Dictionary

Doctrine – That which is taught: The principles, belief, or dogma of any church, sect, or party. Webster's New School & Office Dictionary

Communion – Intercourse; fellowship; common possession; a religious body; partaking of the Eucharist. Webster's New School & Office Dictionary

What a terrible blessing and frightening gift has been given man that he should possess such great capacity to love and such vast ignorance of how to love. What divine urgings drive us to seek out in others that part of Him we so dimly recognize and that our hearts would respond so joyously to His reflection we glimpse in the face of those we love. Oh, feral heart who would settle for the corporeal image but refuse the spiritual source when both are offered so openly. So saddening is the need to touch and feel and taste the beloved that it goads us like animals down the wrong path, settling only for someone to hold and shunning the higher and more pure love of Him who created the very object of our mortal love.

This is a short and barren path, on which we seek love with our whole being and settle for the echo of His voice, heard distorted in the mundane love of this world. Why do we turn our hearts away from the clarion call of God beckoning us home? Possibly it is because we have no insight into what we are missing.

Somehow, our hearts know Him but we cannot see Him. His presence is felt, His spirit is heard, but our eyes are blind, our ears are deaf to the soft rustle of His steps. In the search for love, our hearts frantically scan the faces of those around us. Are you He for whom I search? Are you the Lord? We look into the eyes of everyone passing, testing each one, until we can say, "I look at your face and I see God." But that only happens after we have experienced His presence and recognize it in others.

We await He who is love. Our relationships with others are divinely inspired by the template of God calling us to a communion with Him. God is showing us how we should love Him and be loved by Him. Mortal love falls short, for we desire complete fulfillment only possible with the "Beloved."

Song 1:15 Behold, thou art fair, my love; behold, thou art fair; thou hast doves' eyes. 16 Behold, thou art fair, my beloved, yea, pleasant: also our bed is green. 17 The beams of our house are cedar, and our rafters of fir. 2:1 I am the rose of Sharon, and the lily of the valleys. 2 As the lily among thorns, so is my love among the daughters. 3 As the apple tree among the trees of the wood, so is my beloved among the sons. I sat down under his shadow with great delight, and his fruit was sweet to my taste. 4 He brought me to the banqueting house, and his banner over me was love.

Song 2:10 My beloved spake, and said unto me, Rise up, my love, my fair one, and come away. 11 For, lo, the winter is past, the rain is over and gone;12 The flowers appear on the earth; the time of the singing of birds is come, and the voice of the turtle is heard in our land; 13 The fig tree putteth forth her green figs, and the vines with the tender grape give a good smell. Arise, my love, my fair one, and come away. 14 O my dove, that art in the clefts of the rock, in the secret places of the stairs, let me see thy countenance, let me hear thy voice; for sweet is thy voice, and thy countenance is comely.

Song 5:2 I sleep, but my heart waketh: it is the voice of my beloved that knocketh, saying, Open to me, my sister, my love, my dove, my undefiled: for my head is filled with dew, and my locks with the drops of the night.

Only He can fill our hearts and souls completely. Only in Him can we rest. Only then will our spirits be at peace.

It is not that we do not love friends or family, but there is a higher love and a deeper calling making us know we are not yet fulfilled, not yet at peace, not yet at rest, not yet free of the emptiness that so graciously plagues our souls.

What devastating mercy and vicious grace has been given man that he would receive by some charity of the Spirit of God this disease of sorrow that only God can cure. God places a hook in our hearts and draw us homeward. Here do we have the fisher of men. The great physician and loving Father listens for our call. "Lord, what must I do to be saved?" It is the question that starts the journey of a lifetime as God answers in lessons of love for the rest of our lives.

Acts 16:29 Then he called for a light, and sprang in, and came trembling, and fell down before Paul and Silas, 30 And brought them out, and said, Sirs, what must I do to be saved? 31 And they said, Believe on the Lord Jesus Christ, and thou shalt be saved, and thy house. 32 And they spake unto him the word of the Lord, and to all that were in his house. 33 And he took them the same hour of the night, and washed their stripes; and was baptized, he and all his, straightway.

This relationship is a marriage, mystical and eternal. Christ has assumed his rightful place as both redeemer and husband.

Rev 21:2 And I John saw the holy city, new Jerusalem, coming down from God out of heaven, prepared as a bride adorned for her husband. 3 And I heard a great voice out of heaven saying, Behold, the tabernacle of God is with men, and he will dwell with them, and they shall be his people, and God himself shall be with them, and be their God.

Rev 22:17 And the Spirit and the bride say, Come. And let him that heareth say, Come. And let him that is athirst come. And whosoever will, let him take the water of life freely.

Brethren; I am homesick for a place that I have never been but I know a man who knows the way. W.R. Lumpkin

Thus the lover and the beloved meet in a place known only by them, to be in the presence of one another enabled by Grace, the Grace of the beloved.

COUNT IT ALL GRACE

When starting the mystical journey it may seem appropriate to bring all of your sins of the past up once again before God and confess all you have confessed before. It may seem good to remember yourself in light of how we were as a sinner. All trials and all sins are not only covered under His grace but are part of His grace. This does not diminish our sins in any way. It does not elevate us spiritually one inch, yet it does show us His magnificent and loving heart. For every step and misstep, all pain and tribulation brought us here to His feet and without them we would not be here for such a time as this. Only physical or emotional distress forces us to reconsider our path and only pain of this sort detours us to try other ways. We learn from our mistakes but should not be kept down by them.

We repent and must leave the sorrow of our past deeds behind us.

Don't be troubled when you meditate on the greatness of your former sins, but rather know that God's grace is so much greater in magnitude that it justifies the sinner and absolves the wicked.
Quotations from Cyril of Alexandria (Commentary on the Gospel of St. Luke)

Such a sweet and wonderful balance is maintained between remembering our wretched state and seeking to forget even ourselves in our search for God.

...if any man or woman should think to come to contemplation without many sweet meditations on their own wretched state, on the passion, the kindness and the great goodness and the worthiness of God, they will certainly be deceived and fail in their purpose. At the same time, those men and women who are long practiced in these meditations must leave them aside, put them down and hold them far under the cloud of forgetting, if they are ever to pierce the cloud of unknowing between them and their God.
From The Cloud of Unknowing

I count it all grace that He knew the path of my sinful steps even before He saved me and still, He saved me. I count it all grace that He somehow wove my freewill into His plan, knowing how low and undeserving I am for His love. I count it all grace, my sins, my strengths, my weaknesses, and all of my limitations are counted as a terrible and undeniable gift designed by God to work in conjunction with the path I walk to lead me homeward to Him. Known by God from before the beginning, knitted together in the womb by His hand, blessed with human frailties so deep and pervasive as to have cost the life of God himself, I was led to God's feet.

He who is Love has given me the gift of love. It was given for nothing I have done or been. I was sinful even while confessing my sin. There was no need to beg for love. He loves me more than life. There is nothing I may do to thank Him or repay Him except by my free will to accept this gift He gives that it not be given in vain.

Rom 5:17 For if by one man's offence death reigned by one; much more they which receive abundance of grace and of the gift of righteousness shall reign in life by one, Jesus Christ. 18 Therefore as by the offence of one judgment came upon all men to condemnation; even so by the righteousness of one the free gift came upon all men unto justification of life. 19 For as by one man's disobedience many were made sinners, so by the obedience of one shall many be made righteous. 20 Moreover the law entered, that the offence might abound. But where sin abounded, grace did much more abound: 21 That as sin hath reigned unto death, even so might grace reign through righteousness unto eternal life by Jesus Christ our Lord. 6:1 What shall we say then? Shall we continue in sin, that grace may abound? 2 God forbid. How shall we, that are dead to sin, live any longer therein?

Rom 6:14 For sin shall not have dominion over you: for ye are not under the law, but under grace. 15 What then? shall we sin, because we are not under the law, but under grace? God forbid. 16 Know ye not, that to whom ye yield yourselves servants to obey, his servants ye are to whom ye obey; whether of sin unto death, or of obedience unto righteousness?

For I have attempted to keep myself from sin and sinning and repeatedly failed, utterly. Trying to run or hide from my fallen nature and always finding me with me and never leaving or losing one iota of me, I gave up trying to change me and laid down before Him any hope of my own righteousness. I count myself the only sinner and have received firm rejection from the church, being unable, for any time, to stay me from sinning. Yet, I still feel His spirit welling up within me. But now, there is nowhere to go but to His heart, alone.

You do not have to be perfect. Perfection is not what Christianity is all about. You do your best and God does the "righteousing".   Dr. Gene Scott.

1COR 15:10 But by the grace of God I am what I am: and his grace which was bestowed upon me was not in vain; but I laboured more abundantly than they all: yet not I, but the grace of God which was with me.

2COR 4:14 Knowing that he which raised up the Lord Jesus shall raise up us also by Jesus, and shall present us with you. 15 For all things are for your sakes, that the abundant grace might through the thanksgiving of many redound to the glory of God. 16 For which cause we faint not; but though our outward man perish, yet the inward man is renewed day by day.

JAM 1:1 James, a servant of God and of the Lord Jesus Christ, to the twelve tribes, which are scattered abroad, greeting. 2 My brethren, count it all joy when ye fall into divers temptations; 3 Knowing this, that the trying of your faith worketh patience. 4 But let patience have her perfect work, that ye may be perfect and entire, wanting nothing.

ZEC 4:6 Then he answered and spake unto me, saying, This is the word of the LORD unto Zerubbabel, saying, Not by might, nor by power, but by my spirit, saith the LORD of hosts. 7 Who art thou, O great mountain? before Zerubbabel thou shalt become a plain: and he shall bring forth the headstone thereof with shoutings, crying, grace, grace unto it.

Having been shown His grace, by His grace, I at once saw my shortcomings and needs and was drawn to know a basic wrongness in me. I now hold on with my life, for my life, to the grace of God, knowing He who made me knew me and still loved me enough to woo me, with His prevenient grace, by His spirit, back to Him. And if He could and would do this, that by His longsuffering and forgiveness, He would keep loving me to the very end, seeing that He knew all I would be and do before He saved me. By doing this, He is keeping me for Himself until that day I may be made perfect, over there.

WHAT IS GRACE?

Only by the grace of God can the communion we seek take place. We may ask. We may beg. But, it is only in watchful waiting that we will receive. His grace is sufficient and the only vehicle by which communion with God is granted. But what is grace?

Grace is a blessing, a blessing that is undeserved, unsolicited and unexpected, a blessing that brings a sense of the divine order of things into our lives. The ways of grace are mysterious, we cannot always figure them out. But we know grace by its fruits, by the blessings of its works. We would expect to be startled when grace manifests itself. The opposite is true. It doesn't startle us at all, for grace is everywhere. We may not discern it; we may not recognize it for we are inclined to take it for granted.   "Living with Grace" by Rev. Peter Fleck

If we are walking, dancing, eating, teaching, preaching, meditating, being, we are rid of the impediments which hinder our free movement. We are rid of all the obstacles that block us from being who we are meant to be. This is grace. A grace that indicates not an addition, but rather a subtraction and removal of those things that may hinder us from being who we are. This is grace.   Reverend Bill Clark

Grace "is an attitude on God's part that proceeds entirely from within Himself, and that is conditioned in no way by anything in the objects of His favor." Burton Scott Easton in The International Standard Bible Encyclopedia.

When a thing is said to be of 'grace' we mean that the recipient has no claim upon it, that it was in no-wise due him. It comes to him as pure charity, and, at first, unasked and undesired. A.W. Pink Attributes of God

In a time before his death, Mr. McLaren, minister of the Tolboth church, said, "I am gathering together all my prayers, all my sermons, all my good deeds, all my ill deeds; and I am going to throw them all overboard and swim to glory on the plank of Free Grace."

There is one work which is right and proper for us to do, and that is the eradication of self. But however great this eradication and reduction of self may be, it remains insufficient if God does not complete it in us. For our humility is only perfect when God humbles us through ourselves. Only then are they and the virtue perfected, and not before.
Meister Eckhart

If I were good and holy enough to be elevated among the saints, then the people would discuss and question whether this was by grace or nature and would be troubled about it. But this would be wrong of them. Let God work in you, acknowledge that it is his work, and do not be concerned as to whether he achieves this by means of nature or beyond nature. Both nature and grace are his. What is it to you which means he best uses or what he performs in you or in someone else? He should work how and where and in what manner it suits him to do so.
Meister Eckhart

The self-righteous, relying on the many good works he imagines he has performed, seems to hold salvation in his own hand, and considers Heaven as a just reward of his merits. In the bitterness of his zeal he exclaims against all sinners, and represents the gates of mercy as barred against them, and Heaven as a place to which they have no claim. What need have such self-righteous persons of a Saviour? They are already burdened with the load of their own merits. Oh, how long they bear the flattering load, while sinners divested of everything, fly rapidly on the wings of faith and love into their Saviour's arms, who freely bestows on them that which he has so freely promised!
Jeanne-Marie Bouvier de la Motte-Guyon

Humility is a grace in the soul... It is indescribable wealth, a name and a gift from God. Learn from Me, He said; that is, not from an angel, not from a man, not from a book, but from Me, that is from My dwelling within you, from My illumination and action within you, for I am gentle and meek of heart in thought and in spirit, and your souls will find rest from conflicts and relief from evil thoughts.
John Climacus

Our activity consists of loving God and our fruition of enduring God and being penetrated by his love. There is a distinction between the love and fruition, as there is between God and his Grace.
 John Ruusbroec

Jesus, are you not my mother? Are you not even more than my mother? My human mother after all labored in giving birth to me only for a day or night; you, my tender and beautiful lord, labored for me over 30 years.
Marguerite of Oingt

We are only here and possess what we have because of the timing and grace of God. Whether we have little or we have much, we have it because of God. The love in our hearts and all things we have and feel are because He made us as we are. He sets our path and places us on the path at His time. The people we meet and places we go and thus the situations springing from them are in our lives because we were born for such a time as this. Gratitude keeps our arrogance and pride in check. It assigns all of what we are and all we have to God who made all things and keeps them in existence. Gratitude is the balance point between God and man. Thankfulness is a measure of our dependence on God and our obedience to Him. It is the path that our prayers walk to get to God. Gratitude is how we approach Him.

There are only two things that motivate us to do things: desire and desperation. Gratitude comes from desire. This is the idea of some philosophers, but there is a higher gratitude not understood by the world.

How will I pay back the Eternal
    for all His graciousness toward me?
I will raise the cup of deliverance
    and call out the name of the Eternal.
Psalm 116:12-13 The Voice Bible

There is a gratitude springing from the realization that one has no desires, no needs, nothing lacking. It is gratitude from epiphany. Insight brought on by grace enables us to see how God is providing our path and all things on it. It does not mean we have riches or even health, but that we are where we are supposed to be. Even in our lack or pain, we see somehow we are exactly where God would have us to be.

FROM GOD, CHARITY OF HEART

There are two states in a man's life - love, and a call to be loved. We seek unconditional love because only through this God-like love we rest assured of being accepted with all sins and shortcomings that haunt us every waking hour and in our nightmares. It seems right that we would seek to deliver this kind of love to those closest to us such as our children, spouse, and friends. This kind of love flows from the heart of God. It flows through us to others.

Agape' is the Christian Love as revealed in Jesus. It is spiritual and selfless, and the highest form of human love. It is the kind of love that is spiritual in nature. Agape' is a pure and unselfish love. The writers of the Septuagint use the noun some twenty times, but use the verb form over 250 times. In general terms, the Septuagint translators "invented" a new meaning for agape' by using it to replace the Hebrew "hesed", a word meaning loving-kindness.

Look closely at the difference in translations when it comes to the word agape'.

1COR 13:13 And now abideth faith, hope, charity (agape'), these three; but the greatest of these is charity. 14:1 Follow after charity (agape'), and desire spiritual gifts, but rather that ye may prophesy

1COR 13:13 And now abide faith, hope, love (agape'), these three; but the greatest of these is love (agape')

1COR 8:1 … Knowledge puffeth up, but charity (agape') edifieth. 2 And if any man think that he knoweth any thing, he knoweth nothing yet as he ought to know. 3 But if any man love God, the same is known of him.

1COR 13:1 Though I speak with the tongues of men and of angels, and have not charity, (agape') I am become as sounding brass, or a tinkling cymbal. 2 And though I have the gift of prophecy, and understand all mysteries, and all knowledge; and though I have all faith, so that I could remove mountains, and have not charity (agape'), I am nothing. 3 And though I bestow all my goods to feed the poor, and though I give my body to be burned, and have not charity (agape'), it profiteth me nothing. 4 Charity (agape') suffereth long, and is kind; charity (agape') envieth not; charity (agape') vaunteth not itself, is not puffed up, 5 Doth not behave itself unseemly, seeketh not her own, is not easily provoked, thinketh no evil; 6 Rejoiceth not in iniquity, but rejoiceth in the truth; 7 Beareth all things, believeth all things, hopeth all things, endureth all things. 8 Charity (agape') never faileth:…

So many things flow from the love of God in us. Actions reach out to others in compassion and giving that arise from the impulse of love planted so deeply in our hearts we cannot resist. By these acts, and by this love we shall know we are saved.

1PE 1:22 Seeing ye have purified your souls in obeying the truth through the Spirit unto unfeigned love of the brethren, see that ye love one another with a pure heart fervently: 23 Being born again, not of corruptible seed, but of incorruptible, by the word of God, which liveth and abideth for ever.

OF FLESH, LAW, AND MAN

Mysticism is a direct connection between God and man, and thus must be viewed in this context continually. Man was made for God by God and as such, the fleshly clothing of the body cannot be in enmity with God. For how could Christ offer up to

God anything corrupt? He could not. So if Christ, having been born in the flesh, offered up to God his body as a sacrifice, it becomes obvious the nature of flesh is not corrupt. Unlike the Gnostic and Eastern religions, Christian mysticism does not seek to be free of the fleshy clothing of the body in order to be glorified; instead we seek to be clothed thrice, first in this body, then with the glory of God as He would allow His spirit to reside with us in this earthly tent, and finally with a heavenly garment given us as we are changed to be like Him when we shall see Him.

1JO 3:2 Beloved, now are we the sons of God, and it doth not yet appear what we shall be: but we know that, when he shall appear, we shall be like him; for we shall see him as he is.

The body is not a prison to be endured but a vehicle by which God may be worshiped and praised. Indeed, the flesh, being the same in kind as that of Christ himself, is the temple of the Holy Spirit.

It is therefore not the flesh, which wars against God, but pride and desire and the law of carnality that the flesh obeys. As it has been from his creation, man has obeyed this carnal law and has, through his mortal weakness, turned away from the higher law, which is a spiritual law.

ROM 7:22 For I delight in the law of God after the inward man: 23 But I see another law in my members, warring against the law of my mind, and bringing me into captivity to the law of sin which is in my members.

…This is why they can never be satisfied: They are always hankering after what is finite. But they are infinite in the sense that they will never cease to be, even though because of their deadly sin they have ceased to be in grace.
Catherine of Siena

Desire is a direct result of man's infinitely expanding appetite. Our stomachs, like our carnal souls, stretch to accommodate an ever-growing desire for more, faster, higher, better.
Desire gives way to hunger and a starving man is a fool. Yet, I await Him who will free me from my captivity once and for all. He is my hope, both in glory and in this present time.

This is the way Christians express the Buddhist concept of desire and its spiritually debilitating results.

The lowest carnality, which is pride and is the primal sin, is seen in the desire to "be good" as the law gives zeal to the unenlightened man.

PRO 13:10 Only by pride cometh contention: but with the well advised is wisdom.

PRO 16:18 Pride goeth before destruction, and an haughty spirit before a fall.

1JO 2:16 For all that is in the world, the lust of the flesh, and the lust of the eyes, and the pride of life, is not of the Father, but is of the world.

In pursuit of the letter of the law the foundation and reason of the law is lost beneath man's self-righteousness. The foundation and reason of the law was always love. Love of God and love of one's fellow man is the whole of all law, as stated by Christ. It is also the only thing we cannot "do", since these are internal and attitudinal things springing from one's nature and not one's actions. How could our nature be changed?
Man was given the law by God to force this question to be asked. God becomes the only answer due to man's inadequacies to change his own nature.

Instead of embracing this knowledge and admitting
dependence on God, man turns a blind and prideful eye to the
only law that matters and focuses on those items of action he
can hope to obey. We tithe, go to church, pray before meals,
work in the church, and dress according to church standards.
We know all of the answers in Sunday school, exhibit a never
fading smile, and can defend and explain our theology, but we
do not have love in our hearts and the Spirit of the living God
is not resident in us. This is form without substance; answers
without understanding. It is modern Phariseeism. It is the
antithesis of mysticism. Reliance on intellect and mind is the
enemy of the heart.

1COR 13:3 And though I bestow all my goods to feed the poor,
and though I give my body to be burned, and have not charity,
it profiteth me nothing.

Spiritual pride is the most common form of sin among seekers
and it is one of the main opponents.. It is all-pervasive and is a
direct indication of the flesh rearing its ugly head as we insist
action and law count more than grace and love. Men may be
blind, but God is not. The spirit of the law, which is faith,
humility, and love, will be judged as righteousness. So flesh, in
an attempt to "do" and "act" zealously toward the keeping of
the law, plunges man headlong into spiritual blindness,
thinking, in his pride, man could keep that which is perfect.
Man convinces himself of this but ignoring those areas he
cannot control, such as his own heart, he focuses instead on an
outward show of law and duty. But the law was made to show
man his shortcomings and thus draw him back to Him who is
perfect, the maker and keeper of the law.

LUK 18:11 The Pharisee stood and prayed thus with himself,
God, I thank thee, that I am not as other men are, extortioners,
unjust, adulterers, or even as this publican. 12 I fast twice in
the week, I give tithes of all that I possess. 13 And the

publican, standing afar off, would not lift up so much as his eyes unto heaven, but smote upon his breast, saying, God be merciful to me a sinner. 14 I tell you, this man went down to his house justified rather than the other: for every one that exalteth himself shall be abased; and he that humbleth himself shall be exalted.

It was pride in the angelic host that was the cause and root of sin. It was pride that was propagated into man and caused the downfall. It is pride that controls and blinds us.

ISA 14:11 Thy pomp is brought down to the grave, and the noise of thy viols: the worm is spread under thee, and the worms cover thee.12 How art thou fallen from heaven, O Lucifer, son of the morning! how art thou cut down to the ground, which didst weaken the nations!

GEN 2:25 And they were both naked, the man and his wife, and were not ashamed.3:1 Now the serpent was more subtle than any beast of the field which the LORD God had made. And he said unto the woman, Yea, hath God said, Ye shall not eat of every tree of the garden? 2 And the woman said unto the serpent, We may eat of the fruit of the trees of the garden: 3 But of the fruit of the tree which is in the midst of the garden, God hath said, Ye shall not eat of it, neither shall ye touch it, lest ye die. 4 And the serpent said unto the woman, Ye shall not surely die: 5 For God doth know that in the day ye eat thereof, then your eyes shall be opened, and ye shall be as gods, knowing good and evil. 6 And when the woman saw that the tree was good for food, and that it was pleasant to the eyes, and a tree to be desired to make one wise, she took of the fruit thereof, and did eat, and gave also unto her husband with her; and he did eat.

It continues to be pride that keeps us from seeing the truth of our own nature and existence. Pride and arrogance are grouped together with evil, although we may think evil is on a different and lower level. These four, pride, arrogance, insolence, and evil arise from the same root and are manifestations of the same, all too common, human condition. They all come from putting ourselves first and not understanding we are all equal and the same. We are connected. We are one.

PRO 8:13 The fear of the LORD is to hate evil: pride, and arrogance, and the evil behavior, and vile speech, do I hate.

The root and cause of all four arise from a self-centered viewpoint that takes no one else into consideration. They come from tunnel vision so narrow as to include only the person and his desires. This calls into question the nature of evil. Does evil have a reasoned intent to hurt, kill, and destroy or is there an egomaniacal innocence to evil? Could it be that complete evil is actually a blind selfishness? It is not that the evil man does not make evil plans, he does, but he seldom if ever takes his consequences or the feelings of others into consideration. Only his feelings matter to him. His thoughts and actions are based on fulfilling his own desires at the expense of all others. Feelings and the welfare of others do not come into play, nor do they cross his mind. The nature of evil is a twisted, childish, innocent, self-centeredness.

ISA 14:12 How art thou fallen from heaven, O Lucifer, son of the morning! how art thou cut down to the ground, which didst weaken the nations! 13 For thou hast said in thine heart, I will ascend into heaven, I will exalt my throne above the stars of God: I will sit also upon the mount of the congregation, in the sides of the north: 14 I will ascend above the heights of the clouds; I will be like the most High.

Truth, love, and mercy are found on the path to God. Putting others before oneself, feeling with and for others, seeking the will of God over our own, this is the path to God and the path to truth. Compassion and love give way to mercy and mercy is the essence of grace.

PSA 100:3 Know ye that the LORD he is God: it is he that hath made us, and not we ourselves; we are his people, and the sheep of his pasture. 4 Enter into his gates with thanksgiving, and into his courts with praise: be thankful unto him, and bless his name. 5 For the LORD is good; his mercy is everlasting; and his truth endureth to all generations.

PSA 25:10 All the paths of the LORD are mercy and truth unto such as keep his covenant and his testimonies. 11 For thy name's sake, O LORD, pardon mine iniquity; for it is great. 12 What man is he that feareth the LORD? him shall he teach in the way that he shall choose. 13 His soul shall dwell at ease; and his seed shall inherit the earth.

PSA 26:3 For thy loving kindness is before mine eyes: and I have walked in thy truth. 4 I have not sat with vain persons, neither will I go in with dissemblers. 5 I have hated the congregation of evildoers; and will not sit with the wicked. PSA 31:5 Into thine hand I commit my spirit: thou hast redeemed me, O LORD God of truth.

PSA 85:10 Mercy and truth are met together; righteousness and peace have kissed each other. 11 Truth shall spring out of the earth; and righteousness shall look down from heaven. PSA 100:5 For the LORD is good; his mercy is everlasting; and his truth endureth to all generations. 101:1 I will sing of mercy and judgment: unto thee, O LORD, will I sing.
What is the truth? Jesus Christ is truth.

JOH 1:14 And the Word was made flesh, and dwelt among us, (and we beheld his glory, the glory as of the only begotten of the Father,) full of grace and truth.

A PEOPLE IN ERROR

Why are you proud, dust and ashes?
The Tree of Life by St. Bonaventure

Any relationship based on an exchange of tangibles is only as
stable as the desire or supply of the tangibles. This includes
salvation, heaven, and glory. It is in this simple statement the
failure of "mundane" Christianity rests. Indeed, it is the failure
of all religions that threaten hell and death or offer heaven or
paradise based on conduct. Natural consequences, regret, and
guilt follow actions and those results are enough. This is the
idea of karma expressed in Hinduism and Buddhism.

Devotion based on threat becomes servitude. The devotee
situated as an ox between the carrot of heaven and the goad of
hell is bound to fail just as the ox will tire and fall. But,
devotion springing from a heart of love is not indenturement,
but service gladly given. It is not blackmail but charity. It is not
in seeking the rewards but in seeking God we find the answer.

We must love without motive, and not let this aim in and of
itself become a motive. Love must spring from a pure heart.
Even seeking a pure heart is a motive, which defeats the
purpose of God flowing through us unimpeded by us. To
approach the heart of God is to have God bring us to Him.
Thus, we do nothing but become beggars, waiting for an act of
grace. Rules, doctrine, heaven, and hell do not matter. Church
law and opinion become dung. Our hearts cry out for the
beloved. Only He matters. It is only Him we seek.

Men desire to return to the beloved but the church can no
longer show them the way, only continue to preach moral
lessons and church doctrine, which are as devoid of the
mystical life as the dried bones of a man's corpse.

Like all faiths founded on mystical ideals, Christianity is a heart
condition. It is a relationship. It is a love affair. It is a mystical
and circular relationship of "bringing forth". These are the
three comings of Christ: His incarnation at the crowning of
creation, the second coming when we invite Him into our
hearts, and the third coming is when He comes in glory at the
end of the age. God created man and then became man. Man
submits to God and through God's salvation man brings forth
the spirit of God into this world where it is shared with others.
In time, those with whom we share will also welcome into
themselves the Spirit of God where there will be love and
communion and birth of the spirit of Christ on earth through
them. What could be more intimate than to be made by God
and have God birthed in you? What could be more personal
than the same vows of marriage to love, honor, and obey said
to a Holy and sacred spouse? He is a spouse who knows us
because He made us. He knows us because we live in Him. He
knows us because He lives within us.

We cannot know God through doctrine, although doctrine
attempts in someway to describe, qualify, and quantify God's
laws. This approach is much like using the laws in our legal
system to describe our lifestyle of personal freedom here in the
United States. The confusion arises from the use of the word
"know". There are different levels or ways to "know". One can
know about something or someone by reading a book. This is
knowledge without experience. In the experiencing of the thing
there is a depth and understanding which comes with being in
relationship with the person or thing.

Scripture gives us information and knowledge about God. It
does not give us the experience of God, nor does Scripture give
us a relationship with God. If it did then anyone who read the
Bible would be enlightened. Doctrines are rules and laws
derived from the interpretation of Scripture or assigned as a
rule by a body governing a denomination. Doctrine comes

about for two main reasons; to defend against a heresy, and to describe a difference between theological ideas. In the early days of the church, doctrine was used primarily to defend against ideas the founding fathers saw as antithetical to Christianity. Indeed, much of the New Testament is made up of letters written in part to state and establish doctrine in order to correct error in the church. These are necessary to those who do not understand the idea of Christianity, thinking it is a religion and set of beliefs, or a group of people to be led. Christ himself reduced all doctrine to two phrases.

MAT 22:36 Master, which is the great commandment in the law? 37 Jesus said unto him, "Thou shalt love the Lord thy God with all thy heart, and with all thy soul, and with all thy mind. 38 This is the first and great commandment. 39 And the second is like unto it, Thou shalt love thy neighbour as thyself. 40 On these two commandments hang all the law and the prophets. "

The meaning and implications are obvious. If we have the proper relationship with God and our fellow man we would not need rules.

This is, on the surface, too much to ask of our human nature. It does, however, show us the exact place doctrine plays, or should play, in our religious lives. Even in knowing what is right and wrong, we choose to do what relieves our desires. Knowing the rules, laws, or doctrine does no good since it is beyond our power to do what is right. But the mystical experience will change us.

The other use of doctrine today is to establish a framework of beliefs, which are used to distinguish one denomination from another. Doctrine is like glass, you can see the truth through it but it separates you from the truth. Scripture is not God. Church tradition is not God. They are only reflections and pictures of Him. We may learn of Him through doctrine but that is not the same as knowing Him.

Only in a living, growing relationship can we EXPERIENCE God. This is the only way to KNOW Him. We must now go beyond doctrine into His heart so that we may form a relationship with Him. Doctrine and law become of no consequence when we are obedient to the one who is the source of righteousness.   How can we go against God's law when we are obedient to and guided by the Spirit of God? Yet, should we say we would not sin? Our imperfect and unstable gaze would betray us. But the work of God in us will be seen as we revisit our sins less and less often over longer and longer intervals as He remakes us into His image. The use of doctrine should be limited to assuring we do not stray from this path.

It is because of man's unsteady and skewed gaze that the curse of denominations arose. The very idea that we could see God's entire picture at once, clearly, and in balance speaks to the egotism of man. Denomination can be defined as a focus or obsession on an idea or set of ideas to the point of the imbalance of the whole. Whether it is baptism by water, the faithfulness of God in the face of our faithlessness, the power of the clergy over the members, divorce, works verses grace, predestination verses foreknowledge, who can give communion, or the number of days the baptismal water should be kept, a church may split or denomination may arise over the dispute. Within the church, all denominations arose out of disputation over points of political control, doctrine, or interpretation of scripture, most of which are vain and meaningless. None of which would have happened if the love of God had overcome the love of selfish pride and the search for power.

To keep this kind of conflict from happening in our own hearts, let us put God first. Our theology will become simple and God centered as we turn away from the wisdom and opinions of man. Let us do as Paul said, "For I determined not to know any thing among you, save Jesus Christ, and him crucified. And I was with you in weakness, and in fear, and in much trembling. And my speech and my preaching was not with enticing words of man's wisdom, but in demonstration of the Spirit and of power: That your faith should not stand in the wisdom of men, but in the power of God." 1COR2:2 –5

But, here is the catch – Though we may spend a lifetime endeavoring to understand, reach, meditate, and pray for a moment of unity with God, upon reaching spiritual communion with Him we immediately see He has always been with us and we in Him.

ACTS 17:27 That they should seek the Lord, if haply they might feel after him, and find him, though he be not far from every one of us: 28 For in him we live, and move, and have our being; as certain also of your own poets have said, For we are also his offspring.

JOH 17:19 And for their sakes I sanctify myself, that they also might be sanctified through the truth. 20 Neither pray I for these alone, but for them also which shall believe on me through their word; 21 That they all may be one; as thou, Father, art in me, and I in thee, that they also may be one in us: that the world may believe that thou hast sent me. 22 And the glory which thou gavest me I have given them; that they may be one, even as we are one: 23 I in them, and thou in me, that they may be made perfect in one; and that the world may know that thou hast sent me, and hast loved them, as thou hast loved me.

ROM 8:9 But ye are not in the flesh, but in the Spirit, if so be that the Spirit of God dwell in you. Now if any man have not the Spirit of Christ, he is none of his. 10 And if Christ be in you, the body is dead because of sin; but the Spirit is life because of righteousness. 11 But if the Spirit of him that raised up Jesus from the dead dwell in you, he that raised up Christ from the dead shall also quicken your mortal bodies by his Spirit that dwelleth in you.

CHRIST AND THE INCARNATION

It is at this point we stumble. It is here we fall and fail. It is with words of adoration, love, and the description that we perish in our intent. Even the Holy scriptures, though not in error, because of restrictions of word and language, fall so short as to utterly fail in any possible description of who He is. Here, we destroy our own goals by attempting to somehow qualify or quantify His glory. With any words, no matter how well written, there will be an image formed, an idea set, a concept put in place, all of which will be incomplete and inadequate, and all of which must be transcended and un-known if His fullness is to be tasted.

Anything written will lead the reader into failure of knowing Him completely by placing in our feeble minds some restricted image even if it be holy and powerful. A description is no more the thing being described than a painting is the real sky or sea. One may point to something, describe it in detail, or paint a picture of it and still the image and words are completely useless when compared to the real and authentic item or the experience of the thing. It is more so with God, for He is infinite and cannot be captured in finite language, word, or color. Yet, for those who have not met Him, and for those who know Him only from others, I submit these lines as an enticement in hopes of encouraging you into a personal relationship of communion with Him. We must remember what He said of Himself. "TELL THEM, I AM."

When you hear that Jesus is begotten of God, beware lest the words make some inadequate thoughts of the flesh appear before your mind's eye.
The Tree of Life by St. Bonaventure

GEN 15:1 After these things the word of the LORD came unto Abram in a vision, saying, Fear not, Abram: I am thy shield, and thy exceeding great reward.

EXO 3:13 And Moses said unto God, Behold, when I come unto the children of Israel, and shall say unto them, The God of your fathers hath sent me unto you; and they shall say to me, What is his name? what shall I say unto them?

EXO 3:14 And God said unto Moses, I AM THAT I AM: and he said, Thus shalt thou say unto the children of Israel, I AM hath sent me unto you.

(In the person of Christ} a man has not become God; God has become man. (Cyril of Alexandria: Select Letters)

... for the Only Begotten Word of God has saved us by putting on our likeness. Suffering in the flesh, and rising from the dead, He revealed our nature as greater than death or corruption. What He achieved was beyond the ability of our condition, and what seemed to have been worked out in human weakness and by suffering was really stronger than men and a demonstration of the power that pertains to God. ...This was how He would be revealed as ennobling the nature of man in Himself by making {human nature} participate in his own sacred and divine honors. ... We must not think that He who descended into the limitation of manhood for our sake lost his inherent radiance and that transcendence that comes from his nature. No, He had this divine fullness even in the emptiness of our condition, and He enjoyed the highest eminence in humility,

and held what belongs to him by nature (that is, to be worshipped by all) as a gift because of his humanity.
Cyril of Alexandria

Now, everything is holy which is free of this world's defilement. And {such holiness} is in Christ by His very nature, just as it is in the Father; but in the holy disciples it is something adventitious, introduced from outside {through their participation in the Holy Spirit}, by means of the sanctification that comes by way of grace, and by means of splendid, virtuous living; for this is the manner in which one is fashioned to the divine, supramundane image.
(The Image of God in Man according to Cyril of Alexandria)

Secrets of the incomprehensible wisdom of God, unknown to any beside Himself! Man, sprung up only of a few days, wants to penetrate, and to set bounds to it. Who is it that hath known the mind of the Lord, or who hath been His counselor?
Quotations from Jeanne-Marie Bouvier de la Motte-Guyon

The Incarnation is not a union of wills dependent upon some fragile and inconsistent human response toward Christ. Grace cannot depend upon anything, certainly not the deficiencies of the best of human will. Grace must be unconditional, depending on nothing from, in, or of us. The Incarnation must therefore be an amalgam of Christ with man. This union, although never forced upon us, must be stronger than we and stronger further than any human act or choice. The incarnate Word coming into human conditions and limitations was enacted in order to radically change, alter, and restore us, without destroying us.

God remains God and his man is still man, but after Christ has come upon us we are charged with divine power. Only then are we, the believer, capable of restoring or being restored to the fullness of life as we share in it sacramentally with Him. It then becomes the ultimate paradox that in the strictest

Trinitarian view, God offers praise and prayer to himself through us. But, then, who else would be worthy to praise Him and commune with Him except it be He? God in us as Christ has imbued us with Himself through perfect grace has now made it possible for us to approach the Father in love and adoration.

... He transmits the grace of sonship even to us..., insofar as human nature had first achieved this possibility in Him. (On the Unity of Christ)

It is no longer I who live but Christ who lives in me. We say this, and we read this, but we do not act as if we believe it. We do not understand until His grace floods us and possesses us. It is because we have never sought to be filled to such a degree that only He exists in us.

As we take communion we can meditate on the meaning, for it is the symbol of a mystical experience. It is not the bread that is the Eucharist. It is Christ in us that is the Eucharist, for He is our Thanksgiving, and we are His, and He is the Thanksgiving of God. We should not worry about taking the Eucharist. No one is worthy to partake. The scriptures tell us to partake worthily, the writings do not say to partake if you are worthy. Who is worthy to partake of Christ except Christ alone? We are told that we partake worthily if we discern the body and blood of Christ. Do we know who He is, and why His body and blood were given up? Then we have partaken worthily, because if we know Him, and if He is in us, then it is He who is partaking as only He can partake of something so holy as the body and blood of God Himself.

1COR11:25 After the same manner also he took the cup, when he had supped, saying, This cup is the new testament in my blood: this do ye, as oft as ye drink it, in remembrance of me. 26 For as often as ye eat this bread, and drink this cup, ye do shew the Lord's death till he come. 27 Wherefore whosoever shall eat this bread, and drink this cup of the Lord, unworthily, shall be guilty of the body and blood of the Lord. 28 But let a man examine himself, and so let him eat of that bread, and drink of that cup. 29 For he that eateth and drinketh unworthily, eateth and drinketh damnation to himself, not discerning the Lord's body.

If we could do one small piece to make ourselves worthy, we could not "count it all Grace".
The goodness of man is like children jumping to see who can come closest to the moon. What difference can an inch make in such a shortfall?
Russ Martin

PRESENTING CHRIST IN US TO THE WORLD

Christ has no body now on earth but yours, no hands but yours, no feet but yours, yours are the eyes through which is to look out Christ's compassion to the world: yours are the feet with which he is to go out about doing good; yours are the hands with which he is to bless men now. St. Teresa of Avila

Christ's living in me is at the same time himself and myself. From this moment until I am united with Him in one spirit there is no longer any contradiction implied by the fact that we are different persons. He remains, naturally and physically, the son of God … I remain the singular person that I am. But mystically and spiritually Christ lives in me from the moment that I am united to Him in his death and resurrection…
Thomas Merton

The story of Mary holds within it, several deep lessons for the Christian mystic. Even before the great schism between the Orthodox and Roman churches, Mary held a place in the minds and hearts of the Christian church.

Mercy is not getting the bad consequences that are deserved. Grace is getting the good things we don't deserve. Although it is true grace shed on someone does not indicate moral or spiritual status, it is also true God had a plan for salvation from the foundations of the world and in His plan, Mary had a place. As people of faith, Mary's story has a deep and significant meaning for us. Grace is given without, and many times, in spite of spiritual condition. It was not Mary's state or condition but the willingness of her decision that drew the sovereign will of God. In this vein the early fathers found something so fascinating and deeply spiritual about the story of Mary they elevated her to a venerated status. As we look closer into the story of Mary we will see she is the template and prototype of the true mystical experience. Her experience is the key and summation of the entire Christian process. In her we find our spiritual likeness, our history, and our story. In the story of Mary the mystical life is foretold.

LUKE 1:35 And the angel answered and said unto her, The Holy Ghost shall come upon thee, and the power of the Highest shall overshadow thee: therefore also that holy thing which shall be born of thee shall be called the Son of God. 37 For with God nothing shall be impossible. 38 And Mary said, Behold the handmaid of the Lord; be it unto me according to thy word. And the angel departed from her. 41 And it came to pass, that, when Elisabeth heard the salutation of Mary, the babe leaped in her womb; and Elisabeth was filled with the Holy Ghost: 42 And she spake out with a loud voice, and said, Blessed art thou among women, and blessed is the fruit of thy womb. 43 And whence is this to me, that the mother of my Lord should come to me? 44 For, lo, as soon as the voice of thy salutation sounded in mine ears, the babe leaped in my womb for joy. 45 And blessed is she that believed: for there shall be a performance of those things, which were told her from the

Lord. 46 And Mary said, My soul doth magnify the Lord, 47 And my spirit hath rejoiced in God my Saviour.

LUK 1:48 For he hath regarded the low estate of his handmaiden: for, behold, from henceforth all generations shall call me blessed. 49 For he that is mighty hath done to me great things; and holy is his name. 50 And his mercy is on them that fear him from generation to generation. 51 He hath shewed strength with his arm; he hath scattered the proud in the imagination of their hearts.   52 He hath put down the mighty from their seats, and exalted them of low degree.

Mary was in God's plan for the birth of Jesus before creation, but because of free will she had acquiescence. It was because of her free will and the obedience that followed from it she was blessed. We cannot know why Mary was chosen and set apart. God has always used men and women who seemed common and ordinary to do great things. So it was with the mother of God. Mary, by believing the child in her was indeed sent and fathered by the Holy Spirit of God and set in her virgin body for the redemption of man, became the first Christian.

 The Holy Ghost shall come upon thee, and the power of the Highest shall overshadow thee: therefore also that holy thing which shall be born of thee shall be called the Son of God. Luke 1:35

It was not through doctrine or church that they met but through a real and powerful personal communion. This is the essence of the mystical experience. God draws us and woos us to Him and in our desire to be with Him we are allowed an intimate communion with Him. In this spiritual state of togetherness with God, the Holy Spirit of God implants Christ in our spiritual wombs. Christ forms in us, grows in us, moves in us and through us until we give birth to Him through our hearts and souls and show Him to the world in our love and actions with spontaneous acts of love and serving. It is through a heart and mind that calls out to Him and declares, "Behold the handmaid of the Lord; be it unto me according to thy word." Only in this can we contain God's Spirit. Only in this will God hold us. By this alone comes the world's greatest experience. What we do not realize in our simplicity is each time Christ is birthed in us we are experiencing the mystical equivalent of the incarnation once again. Each time we nurture Him in us and show Him forth to others, we have become Mary and the great incarnation has come upon us.

ISA 9:6 For unto us a child is born, unto us a son is given: and the government shall be upon his shoulder: and his name shall be called Wonderful, Counsellor, The mighty God, The everlasting Father, The Prince of Peace. 7 Of the increase of his government and peace there shall be no end, upon the throne of David, and upon his kingdom, to order it, and to establish it with judgment and with justice from henceforth even for ever. The zeal of the LORD of hosts will perform this.

All of this is beyond logic, beyond reason, beyond explanation. Indeed, it is the mind that fights against the heart of the mystic. Traditional Christians would say it is a matter of faith. That may be so, but it is also a matter of the heart and of intuitively sensing the mystical journey is real and near to us always.

1COR8:1 … Knowledge puffeth up, but charity edifieth. 2 And if any man think that he knoweth any thing, he knoweth nothing yet as he ought to know. 3 But if any man love God, the same is known of him.

2TI 3:7 Ever learning, and never able to come to the knowledge of the truth.

As we seek God we should do so through quiet listening to His spirit in us. We should meditate in His presence. We should pray. We must strive to keep our prayer life in balance between

Discursive prayer and Contemplative prayer. In discursive prayer we carry on a dialogue between the Lord and ourselves. The problem in this type of prayer is we tend to do all of the talking. We bring a wish list before the throne. We repeat our requests as if He did not hear us the first time. We beg God to fill our requests, as if we could possibly know what is best in the light of eternity. We seldom listen to His answer. In contemplative prayer we stay silent and listen to the Lord. We think about Him and His glory. We learn to be still inside so we may hear His soft, beckoning voice.

Prayer is not for us to change the mind of God, but for us to be conformed to His will.

We may seek knowledge but knowledge alone does nothing to change the heart of man or demon. Only being with God and communing with Him will alter our natures and only then according to our ability to yield to His spirit through obedience. Acting on knowledge as truth is faith, and faith is the key to heaven.

Church attendance, obedience to the law, knowledge of the Scriptures, prayers of empty repetition, even worship if it is empty of spirit, will not change the heart of man. Only by being in God's presence can we hope to get to know Him intimately and be changed by exposure to Him; as a child is changed and molded by the parent. Our churches have lost the way back to God. The people are not being told what it takes to live a full spiritual life. Because of this our churches are dying and people are suffering. We go to church, assemble together, read scripture, sing songs, pray, and leave. Seldom, if ever, do we simply sit and wait on the Spirit to come, to speak, to work in us.

TRAPS AND SNARES ALONG THE PATH

Hate, resentment, and anger

As we approach Him we will find our hearts will open to Him and we will begin to recognize His presence in our hearts and lives more easily. We will get to know God on an intimate level. Unfortunately, there are things that will stop us in our tracks. Hate, resentment, and anger can destroy our journey. They are contrary to the heart and wishes of God. These emotions stick like glue to the heart of man. They hang on us like weights around our necks, impeding us on the journey. They will wear us down, fatigue our steps, and halt our progress. Sadly, these things, hate, resentment and anger are some of the last obstacles to be overcome.

Anger: excessive emotion or passion aroused by a sense of injury or wrong; wrath; to provoke to resentment; excite to wrath; enrage.   Webster's New School and Office Dictionary

Hate/Enmity: to dislike intensely: abhor: detest: intense aversion.   Webster's New School and Office Dictionary

Resentment: strong anger or displeasure: deep sense of injury. Webster's New School and Office Dictionary

Hate, anger, and resentment are interwoven emotions. They eat at us and consume us slowly, like an acid; they rot us from the inside. They draw our minds to the pain from injuries done in the past. The pain holds us hostage in the past, by the pain we feel in the present. We hearken to the past and our minds dwell there. Letting go of the pain is not so easy, and although I do not want this to evolve into a book on psychology, we must realize healing and forgiveness are needed.

PHI 2:3 Let nothing be done through strife or vainglory; but in lowliness of mind let each esteem other better than themselves. 4 Look not every man on his own things, but every man also on the things of others. 5 Let this mind be in you, which was also in Christ Jesus:

MAT 5:43 Ye have heard that it hath been said, Thou shalt love thy neighbour, and hate thine enemy. 44 But I say unto you, Love your enemies, bless them that curse you, do good to them that hate you, and pray for them which despitefully use you, and persecute you; 45 That ye may be the children of your Father which is in heaven: for he maketh his sun to rise on the evil and on the good, and sendeth rain on the just and on the unjust.

1JO 3:14 We know that we have passed from death unto life, because we love the brethren. He that loveth not his brother abideth in death.

ROM 12:17 Recompense to no man evil for evil. Provide things honest in the sight of all men. 18 If it be possible, as much as lieth in you, live peaceably with all men. 19 Dearly beloved, avenge not yourselves, but rather give place unto wrath: for it is written, Vengeance is mine; I will repay, saith the Lord. 20 Therefore if thine enemy hunger, feed him; if he thirst, give him drink: for in so doing thou shalt heap coals of fire on his head. 21 Be not overcome of evil, but overcome evil with good.

Anger, strife, and resentment constrict our thoughts and capture them. We dwell on the person that hurt us and not on God. We wish evil on the person. Our pain or anger pulls our thoughts back to him or her constantly. Our imagination runs to hurtful recompense. We become trapped within our malicious thoughts. It is a trap sprung on us by us and it is difficult to escape.

The minimum penalty we can hope for in this state is that our minds will be stripped of God's presence and engorged with resentment and hate. Our beloved will be taken from us by force and replaced with resentment. Our finite minds have only limited capacity and so He will be pushed out when thoughts of anger becomes sizable enough. The intruders will crowd and push the Lord from our heart. Even if some thought of the Lord remains, the voices of hate and anger are strong and constant enough His sweet voice will not be easily heard.

MYSTICISM AND RECIDIVISM

MAT 13:18 Hear ye therefore the parable of the sower. 19 When any one heareth the word of the kingdom, and understandeth it not, then cometh the wicked one, and catcheth away that which was sown in his heart. This is he which received seed by the way side. 20 But he that received the seed into stony places, the same is he that heareth the word, and anon with joy receiveth it;   21 Yet hath he not root in himself, but endureth for a while: for when tribulation or persecution ariseth because of the word, by and by he is offended. 22 He also that received seed among the thorns is he that heareth the word; and the care of this world, and the deceitfulness of riches, choke the word, and he becometh unfruitful. 23 But he that received seed into the good ground is he that heareth the word, and understandeth it; which also beareth fruit, and bringeth forth, some an hundredfold, some sixty, some thirty.

Starting a journey may be easy. Finishing is not. It takes tenacity and a unique stubbornness to complete what is started. The world has tribulations and enticements to sway us from our course. Our roots of desire for God must go deeper than our roots in the world. Although the above passage is usually related to salvation it shows the trials we will go through and has within it a warning. Many fail. Be prepared to endure and push on! Salvation is only the beginning of our journey. Many do not make it to the starting line.

They hear the word and do nothing with it. Then, there are some who receive the word of God and become enlightened. This fully equips us to meet the Lord in heaven, but now, while in this world, we must decide how high up the mountain we wish to climb. Being truthful about ourselves is painful and exhausting. Most will start this mystical journey and grow tired of judging themselves. They will fatigue in seeking God. They will become distracted by the world. They will not endure the Dark Night of the Soul. They will hide their emptiness in the pursuits of this world. They will rest at the foot of the mountain. As for me, I wish to climb the mountain and touch the face of God. It is a costly journey. It will cost time, patience, and finally it will demand from us all we are. But, think of what we will have if we can give it all away.

Most who start this journey will repeat the same step over and over. They will begin, weary, fail, wander, come back, and begin again. Caught in the midst between the emptiness they feel and the price they think they must pay to overcome. Like a seven-day fast they abort after the first day, they will walk the same rutted road again and again. This does no good. It gets us no farther than the time before. Let us make a choice before we begin. After the journey is begun it is either mysticism or recidivism.

From this point on we must live in the present. Those mistakes of the past are now behind us. We are living in the present. We must only think of them to learn from our mistakes. They should in no way hold us back. We cannot cling to them. It would be like holding on to an anchor. They would drag us down. We cannot hope to carry the guilt and shame. They will impede and exhaust us.

If we live in the present there is no past to regret or celebrate. If we live in the present there is no future to dread or desire. Now, the Spirit of God has come to indwell us, teach us, lead us, and change us. Now we can stand before God and commune with Him.

God exists only in the NOW. God is only in the present. We must be here now. This means we can't be held back by regret, guilt, or shame. These things drag our hurting and sorrowful minds back to the past; back to the time and place of the pain. Our minds and hearts must be clear of guilt, shame, and condemnation. The clear and clean eternal now is where our God resides. All paths have led us to this one point in time when we can lay all burdens of regret, guilt, and shame aside.

Now our heart yearns to be with the one who loved us enough to save us. Now we seek the beloved! We must not seek Him in the past. We cannot seek Him in the future. We must seek Him in the present by being totally in the present – here – with Him. He is here in the infinite now.

The past is gone. The future is not yet here. All we have is now. Without looking forward or back, we worship God now. We praise Him for who He is and what is happening now. He is saving us and showering us with His grace, even now. Let us be completely focused on God at this moment, in the ETERNAL NOW.

THE PRESENCE OF GOD

There is the omnipresence of God and the manifest presence of God. Although God is everywhere all the time, we wish His presence manifested in our lives. This can only be done by His grace. With eyes opened and heart on fire we understand the sovereignty of God and cry, "GRACE! GRACE! IT IS BY

GRACE ALONE!" We were wooed, convicted, and saved from condemnation because He is gracious. He did not have to do it. We did not deserve it, but He did it anyway.

Now what God wants is a relationship with us, as a father would want to love and nurture a child. We know God is everywhere but He only reveals Himself as He wishes. He is manifested in our hearts. Visions are splendid, but they pass quickly. Miracles come so seldom. The Christ Spirit is in us forever. It is less spectacular than seeing visions. It is not as awe inspiring as a miracle. The manifest presence of God is when God reveals Himself to us. We may seek those moments of visions and miracles as if they will give us the faith to believe more deeply, but signs will not change a person. Only God in us will do that. This is the most powerful manifest presence of God.

1COR1:22 For the Jews require a sign, and the Greeks seek after wisdom: 23 But we preach Christ crucified, unto the Jews a stumbling block, and unto the Greeks foolishness; 24 But unto them which are called, both Jews and Greeks, Christ the power of God, and the wisdom of God.

A PLACE TO PLACE THE MIND

Thoughts, Actions, and Submission

PSA 63:6 When I remember thee upon my bed, and meditate on thee in the night watches. 7 Because thou hast been my help, therefore in the shadow of thy wings will I rejoice. 8 My soul followeth hard after thee: thy right hand upholdeth me.

PSA 77:12 I will meditate also of all thy work, and talk of thy doings. 13 Thy way, O God, is in the sanctuary: who is so great a God as our God? 14 Thou art the God that doest wonders: thou hast declared thy strength among the people.

At first glance, there is no difference between the meditation techniques of the Zen Buddhist masters and those of the Christian mystics. Both demand the mind be still, quiet, and focused. Both demand we lose ourselves. Both demand patience and dedication. However, there is a distinction between the two as to where the mind is placed. The teaching of the Eastern mystics directs the student to "go within", "empty themselves", and "center the mind". They concentrate on the center of the body or on the breath. First there is focus on sound or breath, then on the center where the breath arrives, and then even that disappears into nothingness until nothing is left, not even the self; not even nothingness. The students reach inside until in the depth all disappears into all and into nothingness.

For the Christian mystic, enlightenment is not nothingness. It is oneness of God and man. We do not seek to disappear but we seek union with Him who is all. Him, together with us, as lover and beloved. Yet, in the end the mystics of all faiths loose themselves in an all-pervasive ocean of divine consciousness.

It is important to still the mind and stop the chaotic ramblings of thoughts so we may be fully attentive to God. We may find it necessary to implement techniques, which will help us clear and fully focus our minds. The two mystical communities of East and West follow similar paths of unity and love. The Christian mystics use the same centering techniques of breath and sound to still and center the mind but the sound is a prayer or word that is meaningful to us in our relationship to God. This may be likened to a mantra.

After the mind is brought under submission the Eastern mystic focuses the mind inward or more specifically on nothing, while the Christian mystic begins to reach toward the heart of God, who is everywhere and nowhere. In both there is a blinding yearning to be one with the all. With Christians it is the spirit of God we seek. With Sufis it is the same. With Hindu and Buddhists it is the all. This may be a difference without a distinction.

We have a longing greater than life. Our heart is a room, a temple built for Him. We are waiting for the guest. It is the longing that does the work. We empty out our ideas of God and of ourselves. We want God to be who He is, not what we think He is. We want His fullness, not our limited idea of His fullness. No idea or imaginings can contain even the slightest portion of Him.

We reach for the Spirit without shape or form. We open the gates of our heart wide in anticipation of the arrival of the beloved. We keep the flame of our heart lit and burning, as one would light a candle to bid someone we love to enter. We wait. We wait. We wait and we reach. We reach until we find our limit. We reach until we find our hearts held down and captive under the cloud that separates us from God. It is then we begin to beat against the cloud with all of the ferocity of a lover held inside a room, away from the beloved, against their will. We have reached as high as we can reach. Like a child who holds up his arms for his father, we wait for God to come, reach down, and pick us up. We wait to be gathered into His arms. Christian Contemplative Prayer is the opening of mind, heart, and soul to God. It is beyond thoughts and words. It is bringing God in us closer than thinking and feeling. The root of all prayer is interior silence. Only mundane and common prayer is of thoughts or feelings expressed in words. Contemplative Prayer is a prayer of silence, an experience of God's presence in us and we in Him. It is experiencing God which transcends the study of Him. Love is an experience.

SONG 1:13 A bundle of myrrh is my well-beloved unto me; he shall lie all night betwixt my breasts. 14 My beloved is unto me as a cluster of campfire in the vineyards of Engedi. 15 Behold, thou art fair, my love; behold, thou art fair; thou hast doves' eyes. 16 Behold, thou art fair, my beloved, yea, pleasant: also our bed is green. 17 The beams of our house are cedar, and our rafters of fir. 2:1 I am the rose of Sharon, and the lily of the valleys. 2 As the lily among thorns, so is my love among the daughters. 3 As the apple tree among the trees of the wood, so is my beloved among the sons. I sat down under his shadow with great delight, and his fruit was sweet to my taste. 4 He brought me to the banqueting house, and his banner over me was love. 5 Stay me with flagons, comfort me with apples: for I am sick of love. 6 His left hand is under my head, and his right hand doth embrace me. 7 I charge you, O ye daughters of Jerusalem, by the roes, and by the hinds of the field, that ye stir not up, nor awake my love, till he please. 8 The voice of my beloved! behold, he cometh leaping upon the mountains, skipping upon the hills. 9 My beloved is like a roe or a young hart: behold, he standeth behind our wall, he looketh forth at the windows, shewing himself through the lattice. 10 My beloved spake, and said unto me, Rise up, my love, my fair one, and come away. SONG 2:11 For, lo, the winter is past, the rain is over and gone; 12 The flowers appear on the earth; the time of the singing of birds is come, and the voice of the turtle is heard in our land; 13 The fig tree putteth forth her green figs, and the vines with the tender grape give a good smell. Arise, my love, my fair one, and come away. 14 O my dove, that art in the clefts of the rock, in the secret places of the stairs, let me see thy countenance, let me hear thy voice; for sweet is thy voice, and thy countenance is comely.

He is illusive. Our God, our lover, entices us to higher levels as we run after Him, seeking Him. We must keep Him in our hearts day and night. When we sleep He is our breath and the beating of our hearts. When awake we are ever watchful. With every fiber of our being we anticipate our next encounter. We wait and our hearts long for Him. The longing draws us to Him.

SONG 3:1 By night on my bed I sought him whom my soul loveth: I sought him, but I found him not. 2 I will rise now, and go about the city in the streets, and in the broad ways I will seek him whom my soul loveth: I sought him, but I found him not. 3 The watchmen that go about the city found me: to whom I said, Saw ye him whom my soul loveth? 4 It was but a little that I passed from them, but I found him whom my soul loveth: I held him, and would not let him go, until I had brought him into my mother's house, and into the chamber of her that conceived me.

We do not turn our minds off, nor do we seek to disappear into nothingness as the Eastern mystics do. We seek Christ, the beloved. We still our hearts and minds to listen for the rustle of His footsteps. We sit quietly, yearning for His approach, His breath upon our face, His fragrance as He enters the room, the mist we see covering His presence, the thin blue mist that surrounds Him. Our minds are turned outward to Him. The more quiet our hearts and minds, the sooner we will recognize Him whom we seek.

TO STILL THE MIND

Let the remembrance of Jesus be present with your every breath. Then indeed you will appreciate the value of stillness. John Climacus

As we begin our time of meditation and prayer we must be careful. We must first still and focus the mind. This first stage, called centering, is somewhat like techniques used in Eastern mysticism, such as Buddhism. However, objects or words used in our Christian technique should be kept completely Christ centered in their representation. As we sit in meditation and prayer, many times we find our minds in turmoil, with thoughts chasing themselves like a pack of monkeys. We must first have a way of clearing the mind of such thrashing. Before we can pray clearly we must be able to think clearly. Before we can think clearly we must stop the mind from running amok. It may take time for the mental dust to settle.

Excerpts from "Five Types of Thought: By Father Thomas Keating

The most obvious thoughts are superficial ones the imagination grinds out because of its natural propensity for perpetual motion. It is important just to accept them and not pay any undue attention to them.... Sometimes they reach a point where they don't hear it at all...

The second kind of thought occurs when you get interested in something that is happening...This is the kind of thought that calls for some "reaction."... It is important not to be annoyed with yourself if you get involved with these interesting thoughts. Any annoyance that you give in to is another thought, and will take you farther away from the interior silence...

A third kind of thought arises as we sink into deep peace and interior silence. What seem to be brilliant theological insights and marvelous psychological breakthroughs, like tasty bait, are dangled in front of our mind's eye... If you acquiesce to a thought of this nature long enough to fix it in your memory you will be drawn out of the deep, refreshing waters of interior silence.

As you settle into deep peace and freedom from particular thoughts, a desire to reflect on what is happening may arise.

You may think, "At last I am getting some place!" or "This feeling is just great... If you let go, you go into deeper interior silence. If you reflect, you come out and have to start over.... As soon as you start to "reflect" on an experience, it is over...The presence of God is like the air we breathe. You can have all you want of it as long as you do not try to take possession of it and hang on to it.

Any form of meditation or prayer that transcends thinking sets off the dynamic of interior purification. One may feel intense anger, sorrow or fear without any relation to the recent past. Once again, the best way to handle them is to return to the sacred word.

Once you grasp the fact that thoughts are not only inevitable, but an integral part of the process of healing and growth initiated by God, you are able to take a positive view of them. Instead of looking at them as painful distractions...
Five Types of Thought: By Father Thomas Keating

It is not that we take a positive approach to the unwanted and noisy thoughts, but we will acquire a passive approach to them. We will learn to dismiss them like twigs on the trail. We will keep walking without as much as noticing them.

...the mind should retire into itself, and recall its powers from sensible things, in order to hold pure communion with God, and be clearly illumined by the flashing rays of the Spirit, with no admixture or disturbance of the divine light by anything earthly or clouded, until we come to the source of the effulgence which we enjoy here, and regret and desire are alike stayed, when our mirrors pass away in the light of truth.
Gregory of Nazianzus

TO QUIET THE MIND

Before we begin the first steps of meditation we must find a
comfortable and undisturbed place. Sit quietly. Close your
eyes and relax. Find in your heart a sacred word. In your heart
and soul it must have a direct connection with Christ. Let the
word be something special to you. Let it be grace, peace, love,
hope, charity, or some word that connects you with Christ
himself. Or, you may pick out some sacred object such as a
cross or painting which you know will draw your heart to Him.
Focus your mind and your heart upon this sacred word or
object. Do not let it waiver and do not let it go.

It is common that after only a matter of moments your mind
will start to wander. You'll find your focus lost, and your mind
chasing itself and swirling like a storm. Your thoughts will
become scattered and chaotic. Do not fret and do not worry,
this is very common. It is the first obstacle to overcome in order
to fully pray and meditate upon Him. God waits on the other
side of chaos in our minds and hearts. This is the first step in
the process of stripping away all of those things that stand in
the way between our Lord and ourselves. The mind will
protest and complain. It is like a stubborn mule which strains
and complains against the bridle. But bridle our minds we
must. It will take infinite time and patience simply to learn to
quiet and control our minds so that we can pray and meditate
wholly on Him.

Why does this little prayer of one syllable pierce the heavens?
Surely, because it is offered with a full spirit, in the height and
the depth, in the length and the breadth of the spirit of the one
who prays. In the height: that is with the full might of the spirit;
in the depth: for in this little syllable all the faculties of the
spirit are contained; in the length: because if it could always be
experienced as it is in that moment, it would cry as it does then;

in the breadth: because it desires for all others all that it desires for itself.... St. John of the Cross

There are only two things in existence, the creator and created. As our minds become more still and quiet we must continually push out all of the things that try to enter in. We must allow room only for God in our hearts and minds. Whether it is height, depth, blackness, emptiness, or nothingness itself, all things but God must be pushed out of the mind and heart.

These two things that exist -- God and creation are all there is in the universe. Everything that is not God is a creation. If we empty our minds and hearts of everything created, even our thoughts, which are created by us, what is left will be God. At this point the children of the book (Jews, Christians and Muslims) arrive at the same place as the Buddhist, Hindu, and secular mystics because they arrive at the same door of nothingness and infinity.

As we focus our minds' eye sharply on the attributes of the ineffable Godhead, we see it as existing beyond everything created. God transcending all intellect, and all beings and is wholly outside any imagined appearance, knowledge and wisdom. "dwelling in light unapproachable."

...it is the easiest exercise of all and most readily accomplished when a soul is helped by grace in this felt desire; otherwise, it would be extraordinarily difficult for you to make this exercise. Do not hang back then, but labour in it until you experience the desire. For when you first begin to undertake it, all that you find is a darkness, a sort of cloud of unknowing; you cannot tell what it is, except that you experience in your will a simple reaching out to God [a naked intent unto God]. This darkness and cloud is always between you and your God, no matter what you do, and it prevents you from seeing him clearly by the light of understanding in your reason, and from experiencing him in sweetness of love in your affection. So set

yourself to rest in this darkness as long as you can, always crying out after him whom you love. For if you are to experience him or to see him at all, insofar as it is possible here, it must always be in this cloud and in this darkness.
Excerpts from The Cloud of Unknowing (James Walsh trans., New York : Paulist Press, 1981)

God is light unapproachable. We cannot gaze on him. We see "in a glass darkly and know in part" (1 Cor 13:12). Deity, God, the Godhead then, is wholly incorporeal, without dimensions or size and not bounded by shape nor perturbed by them.

ROM 8:38 For I am persuaded, that neither death, nor life, nor angels, nor principalities, nor powers, nor things present, nor things to come, 39 Nor height, nor depth, nor any other creature, shall be able to separate us from the love of God, which is in Christ Jesus our Lord.

1 TI 6:16 Who only hath immortality, dwelling in the light which no man can approach unto; whom no man hath seen, nor can see: to whom be honour and power everlasting. Amen.

1 COR 13:12 For now we see through a glass, darkly; but then face to face: now I know in part; but then shall I know even as also I am known.

PHI 3:6 Concerning zeal, persecuting the church; touching the righteousness which is in the law, blameless.7 But what things were gain to me, those I counted loss for Christ. 8 Yea doubtless, and I count all things but loss for the excellence of the knowledge of Christ Jesus my Lord: for whom I have suffered the loss of all things, and do count them but dung, that I may win Christ, 9 And be found in him, not having mine own righteousness, which is of the law, but that which is through the faith of Christ, the righteousness which is of God by faith: 10 That I may know him, and the power of his resurrection, and the fellowship of his sufferings, being made conformable unto his death; 11 If by any means I might attain unto the resurrection of the dead.

Never let the heart cease its cry. Never let it cease its reach for its creator. Day after day this process must be repeated. As we become accustomed to this toil of forgetting all things created, we must continually reach for God with our hearts with every breath we take. Knocking, no, pounding with our heart's cry on the door that stands between God and us. This is called praying without ceasing. Because there is a separation between God and us, it is a great mystery and paradox. Even though He is with us and in us, there stands a veil of "unknowing" whose only key is grace and only door is faith. God himself must lift the veil as He wills.

1TH 5:16 Rejoice evermore. 17 Pray without ceasing. 18 In every thing give thanks: for this is the will of God in Christ Jesus concerning you. 19 Quench not the Spirit. 20 Despise not prophesying. 21 Prove all things; hold fast that which is good. 22 Abstain from all appearance of evil. 23 And the very God of peace sanctify you wholly; and I pray God your whole spirit and soul and body be preserved blameless unto the coming of our Lord Jesus Christ.

In the inner wine cellar I drank of my beloved, and, when I went abroad through all this valley I no longer knew anything, and lost the herd which I was following.
St. John of the Cross

Now I occupy my soul and all my energy is in his service. I no longer tend the herd, nor have I any other work now that my every act is love.
St. John of the Cross

I want to deliberately and zealously encourage a mighty and ongoing longing for God. The lack of it has brought us to our

present low estate. The stiff and wooden quality of our religious lives is a result of our lack of holy desire. Complacency is a deadly foe of all spiritual growth. Acute desire must be present or there will be no manifestation of Christ to His people. He waits to be wanted. Too bad that with many of us He waits so long, so very long, in vain.
A.W. Tozer.

...God is in himself so exalted that he is beyond the reach of either knowledge or desire. Desire extends further than anything that can be grasped by knowledge. It is wider than the whole of the heavens, than all angels, even though everything that lives on earth is contained in the spark of a single angel. Desire is wide, immeasurably so. But nothing that knowledge can grasp or desire can want, is God. Where knowledge and desire end, there is darkness and there God shines.
Meister Eckhart

Desire will drive us to His door, but the door is locked against us. One longs for God and even the longing can keep us from Him. Desire, in itself is a detriment, driving the mind to buck and run like the mule it is. At first, we desire the Lord, seeking Him openly, but if our desire could bring Him to us we would not need grace. There must be nothing of us in this. Our communion with God is in His hands alone. We can have no control in this union except to present ourselves as a willing sacrifice.

At the point we turn it all over to His divine will, God is there, waiting for us. We realize it all depends on His grace. It is because of this paradox we have such turmoil and anguish. It is here the soul is held at a distance from God. The dark night of the soul descends upon us as we work, toil, and suffer to approach Him. Morning comes only when we give up and place even our approach to Him and union with Him in His holy hands.

ROM 11:34 For who hath known the mind of the Lord? or who hath been his counsellor? 35 Or who hath first given to him, and it shall be recompensed unto him again? 36 For of him, and through him, and to him, are all things: to whom be glory for ever. Amen. 12:1 I beseech you therefore, brethren, by the mercies of God, that ye present your bodies a living sacrifice, holy, acceptable unto God, which is your reasonable service. 2 And be not conformed to this world: but be ye transformed by the renewing of your mind, that ye may prove what is that good, and acceptable, and perfect, will of God.

PSA 123:1 Unto thee lift I up mine eyes, O thou that dwellest in the heavens. 2 Behold, as the eyes of servants look unto the hand of their masters, and as the eyes of a maiden unto the hand of her mistress; so our eyes wait upon the LORD our God, until that he have mercy upon us.

1 SA 8:17 And I will wait upon the LORD, that hideth his face from the house of Jacob, and I will look for him.

ISA 40:28 Hast thou not known? hast thou not heard, that the everlasting God, the LORD, the Creator of the ends of the earth, fainteth not, neither is weary? there is no searching of his understanding. 29 He giveth power to the faint; and to them that have no might he increaseth strength. 30 Even the youths shall faint and be weary, and the young men shall utterly fall: 31 But they that wait upon the LORD shall renew their strength; they shall mount up with wings as eagles; they shall run, and not be weary; and they shall walk, and not faint.

God is here when we are wholly unaware of it. He is manifest only when and as we are aware of His Presence. On our part there must be surrender to the Spirit of God, for His work it is to show us the Father and the Son. If we co-operate with Him in loving obedience God will manifest Himself to us, and that manifestation will be the difference between a nominal Christian life and a life radiant with the light of His face. A. W. Tozer

THE DARK NIGHT

In anguish, our soul cries out to God, but He does not answer. In despair we sit alone and empty, in search of Him. We wish to die for Him. We wish to die to self. Our stubborn carnal hearts keep beating. We died because we cannot die. That is to say, we die inside through sorrow because we refuse to die to self. We struggled to lay ourselves down and pick up His Cross, His glory, His life in us. But the old man resists, fighting for each spiritual breath. This "not dying" is agony. We long for Him, waiting for Him with each breath we take, trying to get out of his way. Yet, no matter how we move ourselves we are still in our own way.

The soul cries out but God seems not to hear. Our hearts cry out for the beloved, but He cannot be found. We are poured out like water. Our hearts are like wax melted and running away. We have waited for Him, prayed for Him, meditated on Him, beckoned Him, cried for Him, wept for Him, hurt for Him, and now we are in agony for Him. He is behind the Cloud, we cannot see Him nor can we feel Him. How can one who is everywhere be so far away? But He is. With prayer and desire we beat against the Cloud, the wall that keeps us from God. We cannot get through the wall.

There is no night darker than this. Sorrow is a knife cutting the soul deeper and deeper and so it becomes a bowl, capable of holding more joy when finally there is the joy of His coming. There is no night more sorrowful...but Joy comes in the morning. We can do nothing but to await the beloved. If we endure, this sorrow, this most deep and personal tribulation, will give way to patience and stillness.

LUK 21:19 In your patience possess ye your souls.

Desire will die and obedience will take its place.

ROM 6:16 Know ye not, that to whom ye yield yourselves servants to obey, his servants ye are to whom ye obey; whether of sin unto death, or of obedience unto righteousness?

Grace will be shed on us in obedience to God, and our hearts will receive his fullness.

ROM 5:2 By whom also we have access by faith into this grace wherein we stand, and rejoice in hope of the glory of God. 3 And not only so, but we glory in tribulations also: knowing that tribulation worketh patience; 4 And patience, experience; and experience, hope: 5 And hope maketh not ashamed; because the love of God is shed abroad in our hearts by the Holy Ghost which is given unto us. 6 For when we were yet without strength, in due time Christ died for the ungodly. 7 For scarcely for a righteous man will one die: yet peradventure for a good man some would even dare to die. 8 But God commendeth his love toward us, in that, while we were yet sinners, Christ died for us. 9 Much more then, being now justified by his blood, we shall be saved from wrath through Him.

…with no other light or guide than the one that burned in my heart.
The Dark Night by St John of the Cross

Where have you hidden, Beloved, and left me moaning? You fled like the stag after wounding me; I went out calling you but you were gone.

Spiritual Canticle by St John of the Cross.

God, who is all perfection, wars against all imperfect habits of the soul, and, purifying the soul with the heat of his flame, he approves its habits from it, and prepares it, so that at last he may enter it and be united with it by his sweet, peaceful, and glorious love, as is the fire when it has entered the wood.
St. John of the Cross

What satisfies love best of all is that we be wholly stripped of all repose, whether in strangers, or in friends, or even in love herself. And this is a frightening life love wants, that we must do with the satisfaction of love in order to satisfy love. They who are thus drawn and accepted by love, and fettered by her, are the most indebted to love, and consequently they must continually stand subject to the great power over strong nature, to content her. And that life is miserable beyond all that the human heart can bear.
Hadewijch of Antwerp

Our task is to offer ourselves up to God like a clean smooth canvas and not bother ourselves about what the God may choose to paint on it, but, at every moment, feel only for stroke of his brush. It is the same piece of stone. Each blow from the chisel of the sculptor makes it feel -- if it could feel -- as if it were being destroyed. As blow after blow rings down on it, the stone knows nothing about how the sculptor is shaping it. All it's feels is the chisel hacking away at it's, savaging it and mutilating it.
Jean Pierre Caussadede

When God is seen in darkness it does not bring a smile to the lips, nor devotion, or ardent love; neither does the body with the soul tremble or move as at other times; the soul sees nothing and everything; the body sleeps and speech is cut off. Angela of Floigno

NO PLACE FOR EGO

We are separate and individual creatures, wishing to fit in, wishing to be unique, wishing to be united, wishing to be distinct. We vacillate between the positions, thinking they are opposites. They are not. The wall in our psyche allowing us to distinguish ourselves from others around us is called the ego boundary. Our egos stubbornly refuse to yield, even to God. Pride and self-protection keeps us separate and distinct but we are not complete or whole. The effects of breaching the ego boundary can be seen in those moments of spiritual or sexual bliss. In the union of husband and wife, in those moments of complete tenderness and giving, when distinction between the lover and beloved is lost, and for a space of time it becomes impossible to know where the emotional and physical lines exist between you and the other. There is no fear of losing self but instead a sense of being poured into the other body and soul in a union both separate and together; individual and united, resulting in tears of joy and a river of emotional release as one is being cleansed as if a flood was washing through the soul.

So it is with the union of God and man. When man's ego boundary is finally lowered and man gives himself, even his self-hood, completely up to God. Man and his individuality are not lost but are borne upon the wings of God's love, washing man clean in a river of love. Breaching the ego boundary is a spontaneous act uncontrolled by man. It is made possible by trust and love deep enough to surrender life and self.

Joseph Lumpkin

BEING BOUND TOGETHER WITH GOD

Bind us together, Lord. Bind us together with cords that cannot be broken.
From a spiritual song.

The eyes of my soul were opened, and I beheld the plenitude of God, wherein I did comprehend the whole world, both here and beyond the sea, and the abyss, and the ocean, and all things. In all these things I beheld naught save the Divine power, in a matter assuredly indescribable; so that through excess of marveling the soul cried with a loud voice, saying, "this whole world is full of God!" ....
Angela of Floigno

Yet the creature does not become God, for the union takes place in God through Grace and our homeward turning love: and therefore the creature in its inward contemplation feels the distinction and the otherness between itself in God.
John Ruusbroec

To come into His presence we have Love, Praise, and Gratitude. When all three of these attributes are brought to bear in one relationship there is fullness and joy.

Out of the three, gratitude is the most overlooked. In our world we arrogantly presume our looks, intelligence, strength, or cunning are the reasons we have success, house, car, job, health, or position. We are fools. Without thankfulness we come to believe we sustain ourselves by our own hands. What we have and what we believe we deserve takes on larger proportions and greater value than it should. We come to worship the things of this world more than the maker of all things.

85

Gratitude is pure prayer. In a state of gratitude there is no need to mumble words, for our heart is already dancing before God. How could we pray with words? They would fall short of the song our soul sings.

But, with a heart open and grateful to God we have joy and an enduring relationship.

PSA 100:2 Serve the LORD with gladness: come before his presence with singing. 3 Know ye that the LORD he is God: it is he that hath made us, and not we ourselves; we are his people, and the sheep of his pasture. 4 Enter into his gates with thanksgiving, and into his courts with praise: be thankful unto him, and bless his name. 5 For the LORD is good; his mercy is everlasting; and his truth endureth to all generations. 101:1 I will sing of mercy and judgment: unto thee, O LORD, will I sing.

Out of gratitude and love springs charity. Charity flies forth from a heart filled with thankfulness and gratitude. All things are seen, as they are, a gift from God. We clearly see His love for us. Our hearts are joyous as we share God's gifts to us with others. Charity is the result of gratitude to God and God's love in us toward our fellow man.

COL 3:14 And above all these things put on charity, which is the bond of perfectness. 15 And let the peace of God rule in your hearts, to the which also ye are called in one body; and be ye thankful.

1 COR 13:13 And now abideth faith, hope, charity, these three; but the greatest of these is charity.

What is the secret of finding the treasure? There isn't one. The treasure is everywhere. It is offered to us at every moment and wherever we can find ourselves. (In) All creatures, friends or enemies, for it is ours abundantly, and it courses through every

fiber of our body and soul until it reaches the very core of our being. If we open our mouths they will be filled.
Jean Pierre Caussadede

Fickle and forgetful is man that he would trip over the truth, or through grace fall headlong into it, and then rush off, forgetting all he had seen, learned, and felt in his deepest part. Not being reminded of the epiphany daily, man creeps into a mode of doubt and counts all of his communion and time with God as the dross of dreams and imaginings. In the dark nights of the soul, it is not knowledge that keeps us alive. It is faith, unshakable and tenacious. Faith trusts God is still there even if He cannot be seen. Faith knows God is there even if He cannot be felt. Faith sees the sun in the midst of night and faith waits, for Joy comes in the morning. Do you have knowledge of this faith? Is your heart fixed on God? Then the bridegroom will come and we will be one, transformed and conformed, we will be one.

PSA 57:7 My heart is fixed, O God, my heart is fixed: I will sing and give praise. 8 Awake up, my glory; awake, psaltery and harp: I myself will awake early. 9 I will praise thee, O Lord, among the people: I will sing unto thee among the nations. 10 For thy mercy is great unto the heavens, and thy truth unto the clouds. 11 Be thou exalted, O God, above the heavens: let thy glory be above all the earth.

But what passes in the union of the Spiritual Marriage is very different. The Lord appears in the centre of the soul, not through an imaginary, but through an intellectual vision ..., just as He appeared to the Apostles, without entering through the door, when He said to them: "Pax vobis" (peace be unto you) the soul, I mean the spirit of this soul, is made one with God, Who, being likewise a Spirit, has been pleased to reveal the love that He has for us by showing to certain persons the extent of that love, so that we may praise His greatness. For He

has been pleased to unite Himself with His creature in such a way that they have become like two who cannot be separated from one another: even so He will not separate Himself from her.
Teresa of Avila

... it must not be thought that the faculties and senses and passions are always in this state of peace, though the soul itself is. In the other Mansions (i.e. those mansions which are exterior to the central one in which the soul now dwells) there are always times of conflict and trial and weariness, but they are not of such a kind as to rob the soul of its peace and stability -- at least, not as a rule. ...for it is difficult to understand how the soul can have trials and afflictions and yet be in peace...
Teresa of Avila

... in this temple of God, in this Mansion of His, he and the soul alone have fruition of each other in the deepest silence. There is no reason now for the understanding to stir, or to seek out anything, for the Lord Who created the soul is now pleased to calm it and would have it look, as it were, through a little chink, at what is passing. Now and then it loses sight of it and is unable to see anything; but this is only for a very brief time
Teresa of Avila

And I am quite dazed myself when I observe that, on reaching this state, the soul has no more raptures (accompanied, that is to say, by the suspension of the senses), save very occasionally, and even then it has not the same transports and flights of the spirit. These raptures, too, happen only rarely, and hardly ever in public as they very often did before. Nor have they any connection, as they had before, with great occasions of devotion...
Teresa of Avila

It is the nature of the Holy Spirit that I should be consumed in him, dissolved in him, and transformed wholly into love. ...

God does not enter those who are freed from all otherness and all createdness: rather he already exits in an essential manner within them...
Meister Eckhart

God is always near you and with you; leave Him not alone. ...I continued some years, applying my mind carefully the rest of the day, and even in the midst of my business, to the presence of God, whom I considered always with me, often in me.
Brother Lawrence

... And the latter (union) comes to pass when the two wills -- namely that of the soul and that of God -- are conformed together in one, and there is naught in the one that is repugnant to the other. And thus, when the soul rids itself totally of that which is repugnant to the Divine will and conforms not with it, it is transformed in God through love.   Saint John of the Cross
In thus allowing God to work in it, the soul ... is at once illumined and transformed in God, and God communicates to it His supernatural Being, in such wise that it appears to be God Himself, and has all that God Himself has. And this union comes to pass when God grants the soul this supernatural favour, that all the things of God and the soul are one in participant transformation; and the soul seems to be God rather than a soul, and is indeed God by participation; although it is true that its natural being, though thus transformed, is as distinct from the Being of God as it was before...
Saint John of the Cross

JOH 14:18 I will not leave you comfortless: I will come to you. 19 Yet a little while, and the world seeth me no more; but ye see me: because I live, ye shall live also. 20 At that day ye shall know that I am in my Father, and ye in me, and I in you. 21 He that hath my commandments, and keepeth them, he it is that loveth me: and he that loveth me shall be loved of my Father, and I will love him, and will manifest myself to him.

JOH 15:4 Abide in me, and I in you. As the branch cannot bear fruit of itself, except it abide in the vine; no more can ye, except ye abide in me. 5 I am the vine, ye are the branches: He that abideth in me, and I in him, the same bringeth forth much fruit: for without me ye can do nothing.

To abide in the one we love, what bliss this is. In the sense of husband and wife and as lover and beloved, to be in the presence of the one whom your soul loves heals and extends the soul. It fills and fulfills the soul and by this there is no more need for expressions of ecstasy because ecstasy is here. Expressions of ecstasy come as we are reaching for or entering it. When there, we become quiet and peaceful, wanting nothing more than to remain. To stay, to look upon the face of the beloved, to remain in the embrace, being bound together with God brings peace passing all understanding.

The contemplative life in a modern world is one of walking introspection and self-observation. As we come to understand how truly sinful we are, we also come to understand the vastness of His grace and gift to us. As we watch our thoughts and actions closely and ask why we act and think as we do we will see all we are grows from a root of selfishness and pride. Yet, as we watch these flaws and acknowledge them they will begin to disappear.

The contemplative life in this rushed and demanding world is one of continual prayer and upward reaching to God. There is wisdom in not relying on our own knowledge and abilities. There is wisdom in insecurity. We cannot assume we understand the heart and mind of God. We must continue to seek Him and seek His wisdom for us.

PRO 3:5 Trust in the LORD with all thine heart; and lean not unto thine own understanding. 6 In all thy ways acknowledge him, and he shall direct thy paths. 7 Be not wise in thine own eyes: fear the LORD, and depart from evil.

There are none more dangerous than people or denominations who believe they have the entire truth. There are none so proud and in error as those who believe they have the only way. If a church believes they are "The Way" they have supplanted even Christ.

JOH 14:6 Jesus saith unto him, I am the way, the truth, and the life: no man cometh unto the father, but by me. 7 If ye had known me, ye should have known my Father also: and from henceforth ye know him, and have seen him.

The contemplative person seeks God and not some "way". He seeks to know and love God more each day. It is not about some formula of baptism, names, titles, or membership. It is about seeking the face of God.

This contemplative life demands patience. We rely on the grace of God. Although we continually knock on the door of heaven with the urgings of our heart toward Him, it is up to God to open the door. We never know when we will knock and grace will open the door. We never know what God has in store for us when grace opens the door. It could be a calming breeze to our soul, a vision of hell, or God's overwhelming presence.

Visions may be an expression of what the spirit can communicate in no other way. Certainly, there would be no need for visions and dreams if we were fully aware of those things of God. If we were fully His or could see Him or hear Him we would know those things which visions reveal to our dull hearts and minds. Visions are gifts for those who could not see any other way.

Visions are God's picture book for us, just as we had in
kindergarten.
Wanda Adam

We never know when we will be surprised by grace. Even if it
never happens He is still God. We may never hear His voice or
sense His presence, but He is still God. To know this is to live
in Him. To recognize it is to have the manifest presence of God
in our life.

In this life where we seek the love of God, we may meet Him
along the way from time to time. When man meets God he is
changed forever, but even if he does not meet God in a
manifest way, man is still changed because God is slowly
working in a personal way within our hearts right now. To be
completely aware of His presence in our life will have the same
effect as any manifestation because at that moment of
realization He is manifest to you. The realization of God is the
manifestation of God. Although it may not be in pillars of
smoke and fire, we see Him in our lives, in our hearts, and in
our world. Our souls exclaim:

PSA 8:1 O LORD, our Lord, how excellent is thy name in all
the earth! …

This is not to be found in the "religious" life. Liturgy,
ceremony, repetition, prayers, yantra, mantra, movement, nor
deprivation will bring us one step closer to Him. He is found in
the searching. He is found in the desire to know Him. He is
found in the depth of our love of Him.

(Those who would be partakers of eternal life) must further
possess a vigilant and wakeful mind, distinguished by the
knowledge of the truth, and richly endowed with the radiance
of the vision of God; so as for them, rejoicing therein, to say
Thou, O Lord, will light my lamp: Thou, my God, wilt lighten
my darkness .

Cyril of Alexandria

... It is our duty, therefore, to draw near to the true light, even Christ, praising Him in psalms and saying, Lighten mine eye, that I sleep not for death... Let, therefore, our loins be girt, and our lamps burning, according to what has been spoken unto us.
Cyril of Alexandria

(The Son) Himself shed the divine and spiritual light on those whose heart was darkened; for which reason He said, I am come a light into this world).
Cyril of Alexandria

Oh, union of unity, demanded of God by Jesus Christ for men and merited by him! How strong is this in a soul that is become lost in its God! After the consummation of this divine unity, the soul remains hid with Christ in God. This happy loss is not like those transient ones which ecstasy operates, which are rather an absorption than union because the soul afterwards finds itself again with all its own dispositions. Here she feels that prayer fulfilled -- John 17:21: "That they all may be one as thou Father art in me, and I in thee; that they also may be one in us."
Jeanne-Marie Bouvier de la Motte-Guyon

PSA 8:1...who hast set thy glory above the heavens.

PSA 18:46 The LORD liveth; and blessed be my rock; and let the God of my salvation be exalted.

PSA 34:3 O magnify the LORD with me, and let us exalt his name together.

PSA 34:8 O taste and see that the LORD is good: blessed is the man that trusteth in him.

PSA 40:1 I waited patiently for the LORD; and he inclined unto me, and heard my cry. 2 He brought me up also out of an horrible pit, out of the miry clay, and set my feet upon a rock, and established my goings. 3 And he hath put a new song in my mouth, even praise unto our God: many shall see it, and fear, and shall trust in the LORD.

ISA 40:31 But they that wait upon the LORD shall renew their strength; they shall mount up with wings as eagles; they shall run, and not be weary; and they shall walk, and not faint. 41:1 Keep silence before me, O islands; and let the people renew their strength:

We have examined the words of some of the greatest Christian mystics using their own words. These words give light to their path. It is the same path traveled by mystics from the beginning of mankind.

Let us not view religions or denominations as exclusive based on the fact that they have different terms and names. Whether one worships God or Allah, whether one believes the spokesman of god was Jesus, Muhammad, or Buddha, if we believe there is one divine, one creative force, one spirit, one universal mind, then we are seeking the same One – the same God.

Each religion and discipline may have its own language but they are only words pointing to the same experience and way. In the end, there is the ALL, the ONE, and there is LOVE

Is this not the mystical life? Is this not the life we seek?

The Link Between Zen and Christianity

The connections between Buddhism and Christianity go back many centuries. Laypeople may focus on the numerous superficial differences, but the monks appreciated the similarities. Mutual respect developed between the 6th century masters of China and Brother Adam, a Christian priest, resulting in Brother Adam being enlisted to assist in translating an important religious document or sutra.

Much of the history of this era is missing but we do have a few insights as to how the joint translation occurred. It was in the latter part of the reign of Emperor Dezong and through the 780s that the connections between the emperor, his courtly eunuchs, and generals were forged with Buddhism in a political way. The resulting "theocracy" linked Esoteric Buddhist tradition to intrinsic connections between emperor, court and clergy, — eventually leading to a priest in the Church of the East Metropolitan named Adam assisting translating The Sūtra of the Six Mahāyāna Pāramitās with Esoteric master Prajña.

When Emperor Dezong first came to the throne, he attempted to control the influence of eunuchs within the government and military. At this time the emperor was more favorable toward Daoism than Buddhism. He saw this as a way of returning the Tang Empire and what he saw as its native Chinese spiritual and political resources. He assumed this would bring the empire stability following the An Lushan Rebellion. He was incorrect. It was through a complicated history of uprisings, rebellions, and political maneuvers that swung the emperor toward Buddhism and led to the meeting of Adam and Prajña. The meeting gave way to the decision for Adam and Prajña to work together. Though the project may initially have come from the court's eunuchs (generals of the military), it was likely viewed favorably by the imperial household, the Esoteric clerical establishment, and the Church of the East at once.

It seems the landmark religious endeavor had its roots in politics, and thus it is with much of the world's religious evolution.

The eunuchs approached the Church of the East with a scheme to work together with an Esoteric Buddhist master with known connections to the same groups of foreign fighters to which the Church of the East belonged, and in order to present a translation of an Esoteric Buddhist text containing prayers enabling the emperor to protect his kingdom through the invocation of Tantric deities. The jointly translated sutra lost some of its more esoteric Buddhist flavor, which was replaced with Adam's Christian perspective.

Latter the process would be reversed when the Apostle Thomas ventured into India and to the East. Upon his return he wrote, "The Gospel of Thomas," which has a distinctly eastern flavor and in fact may be the oldest gospel. Because of the eastern tone the church fathers labeled the gospel as Gnostic and excluded it from the Bible.
(A translation of the Gospel of Thomas can be obtained from Fifth Estate Publishing.)

Others journeyed from west to east and wrote about religion and philosophy, but the greatest of these was Thomas Merton. Merton was a Trappist Catholic monk who went to Japan in search of spiritual insights that might deepen his personal spiritual journey. He compared the journey and practices of Christian monks with those of Zen Buddhist monks.

In Merton's book, Mystics and Zen Masters, he says of Zen that it is " a concrete and lived ontology which explains itself not in theoretical propositions but in acts emerging out of a certain quality of consciousness and awareness. Only by these acts and by this quality of consciousness can Zen be judged." Merton thought Zen compatible with Christianity. In its essence Buddhism is about suffering, its causes, and how to live beyond it. It is about emptiness (the delusion of a subject-object distinction and the non-substantiality and transient nature of all existence). It is also about universal compassion. Merton approved of Suzuki's comment that the most important thing is love.

Merton, then, argues that Christian mystics approach (in the apophatic tradition of approaching God with no words or images) the void, emptiness, the transcendence of subject and object, in their sense of pure darkness (the dark night of the soul and of the senses of John of the Cross), kenosis and abandonment. For them, too, pure void and pure light come together. Merton cites John of the Cross' enigmatic remark about todo y nada (everything and nothing at once!). He also lifts up the remark of the mystic Jacob Boehme: " God is called the seeing and finding of the Nothing and, therefore, is called a nothing (though it is God himself) because it is inconceivable and inexpressible." Again, he found affinities to Zen in the remarks of Meister Eckhart: " To be a proper abode for God and fit for God to act in, a man should be so poor that he is not and has not a place for God to act in. To reserve a place would be to maintain distinctions."

Merton had a very strong attraction to Zen. In his lecture, " Monastic Experience and East-West Dialogue", delivered in Calcutta shortly before he died, Merton said: " I come as a pilgrim who is anxious to obtain not just information, not just ' facts' about other monastic traditions but to drink from ancient sources of monastic vision and experience. I seek not to just learn more quantitatively about religion and monastic life but to become a better and more enlightened monk (qualitatively) myself." Again in Zen and the Birds of Appetite Merton argues: " Both Christianity and Buddhism show that suffering remains inexplicable, most of all for the man who attempts to explain it in order to evade it, or who thinks explanation itself is an escape. Suffering is not a ' problem' as if it were something we could stand outside of and control. Suffering, as both Christianity and Buddhism see, each in its own way, is part of our very ego-identity and empirical existence, and the only thing to do about it is to plunge right into the middle of contradiction and confusion in order to be transformed by what Zen calls ' the great death' and Christianity calls ' dying and rising with Christ'. "

In his Calcutta talk, Merton affirmed: " I think that we have now reached a stage of religious maturity at which it may be possible for someone to remain perfectly faithful to a Christian and Western monastic commitment and yet learn, in depth, from a Hindu or Buddhist discipline or experience. Some of us need to do this in order to improve the quality of our own monastic life.". Merton told Brother David Steinal-Rast, shortly before Merton died: " I do not believe that I could understand our Christian faith the way I understand it if it were not for the light of Buddhism."

Before he died, Merton undertook an Asian journey to Bangkok, India and Sri Lanka. He spent three successive days in conversation with the Dalai Lama. The latter said of Merton that he was a kind of Christian geshe, (geshe means "virtuous friend". It is a title reserved for Tibetan Buddhist monks and nuns who are academics.) He also said that in Merton he had met for the first time a Christian spiritual man who opened his own eyes to what could be learned also by Buddhism from the west (The Dalai Lama underscored social service and its connection to contemplation). Merton's last journal, The Asian

Journal of Thomas Merton, recounts in detail his sense that the dialogue with Buddhism was not to become some facile syncretism and did involve a scrupulous respect for important differences. Yet he had found in Suzuki, the Dalai Lama and the Vietnamese Buddhist monk, Thich Nhat Han, sources to help him drink from this ancient source and yet remain a Catholic monk.

In the teachings of Christianity, which I take to include such noncanonical works such as the Gospel of Thomas, the notion of 'light' plays a preeminent role is understanding the heart of Christianity. With regard to the Zen of Christianity, like in Buddhist Zen, all activity is a revelation of spiritual light.

"It is I who am the light which is above them all. It is I who am the all. From me did the all come forth, and unto me did the all extend. Split a piece of wood, and I am there. Lift up the stone, and you will find me there" (The Coptic Gospel of Thomas).

In the Zen of Christianity, spiritual light is active and animative. It is understood to be tabernacled in the flesh; although not being born of the flesh. Rather, this light comes from the highest which cannot even be described as God. Any attempt to describe this spiritual light is really an attempt to materialize the absolute which is immaterial like the Buddhist 'Tathagata' (Lit., coalesced with thatness).

For one who actualizes this light, in which it is distinguished from the flesh, he or she can be said to behold the Christ, which in Buddhism is called abhisheka, literally meaning 'anointed'.

According to the Mahayana Buddhist canon, when an anointed Bodhisattva reaches the last stage of perfection which is called the dharmamegha, roughly meaning "cloud of the dharma", he acquires a body of light. Such a body emits rays which destroy pain and misery when we witness it directly. This same body also performs many miracles. Such, is also the true body of Christ which Jesus realized. Jesus, in this sense, is a Jewish Buddha who has come into the world to remove the suffering of the multitudes (i.e., sentient beings).

Because the many sense his light inasmuch as Jesus is anointed by the light, they are freed from sin, that is, they are freed from further attachment to the corporeal body which leads to suffering. Before they saw Jesus the Anointed, they were like the dead. After they beheld the light, they were raised from the deathlike sleep of material life. This is called, in Greek, Anastasis, translated as 'resurrection' which is the same as Bodhi or awakening. Those who are awakened, are thus able to realize the true heavenly kingdom or, the same, the Buddhist kingdom of light, Svarga.

For anyone who really knows the purport of Zen, it is easy to see it in Christianity and especially in Gnostic Christianity.

Thomas Merton, had ventured to Japan and trained in Zen Buddhism. He meditated and lived with the monks there. His comparison between Christian monks and Zen monks yielded the following observations:

Thomas Merton Quotes- Mystics and Zen Masters
Merton, Thomas. Mystics and Zen Masters. New York: Noonday Press, 1996.

"Buddhism is generally described in the West as 'selfish,' even though the professed aim of the discipline from the very start is to attack and overcome that attachment to individual self-affirmation and survival which is the source of every woe." (8)

"What, exactly, is Zen? If we read the laconic and sometimes rather violent stories of the Zen masters, we find that this is a dangerously loaded question: dangerous above all because the

Zen tradition absolutely refuses to tolerate any abstract or theoretical answer to it. In fact, it must be said at the outset that philosophically or dogmatically speaking, the question probably has no satisfactory answer. Zen simply does not lend itself to logical analysis." (12)

"Zen enlightenment is an insight into being in all its existential reality and actualization. It is fully alert and superconscious act of being which transcends time and space." (17)

"Zen insight is not our awareness, but Being's awareness of itself in us." (17)

"Zen could not be found merely by turning away from active life to become absorbed in meditation. Zen is the very awareness of the dynamism of life living itself in us- and aware of itself, in us, as being the one life that lives in all." (22)

"Zen is not 'attained' by mirror-wiping meditation, but by self-forgetfulness in the existential present of life here and now. This reminds us of St. John of the Cross and his teaching that the 'Spiritual Way' is falsely conceived if it is thought to be denial of flesh, sense, and vision in order to arrive at higher spiritual experience. On the contrary, the 'dark night of sense' which sets the house of flesh at rest is at best a serious beginning. The true dark night is that of the spirit, where the 'subject' of all higher forms of vision and intelligence is itself darkened and left in emptiness: not as a mirror, pure of all impressions, but as a void without knowledge and without any natural capacity to know the supernatural. It is an error to think that St. John of the Cross teaches denial of the body and the senses as a way to reach a higher and more secret mystical knowledge. On the contrary, he teaches that the light of God shines in all emptiness where there is no natural subject to receive it. To this emptiness there is in reality no definite way.

'To enter upon the way is to leave the way,' for the way itself is
emptiness." (25-26)

"The ideogram which represents Tzu, in Lao Tzu (Master Lao),
means both 'master and child.' Indeed, we find this ideogram
combined with another in the word hsiao, meaning filial love.
There the 'son' is seen bearing the 'father' on his shoulders. A
master is therefore a child of the ancient Fathers, who bears
their tradition with him and transmits it to future generations.
Or rather, to be much more accurate, a master is a child who,
like Lao Tzu, knows how to draw secret nourishment in silence
from his 'mother' the Tao. Hence, we see that a master is not
merely one who learns and repeats authoritative forms of
words passed on from the time of the ancients; he is one who
has been born to his wisdom by the mysterious all- embracing
and merciful love which is the mother of all being. He is one
who knows the unknown not by intellectual penetration, or by
a science that wrests for itself the secrets of heaven, but by
wisdom of 'littleness' and silence which knows how to receive
in secret a word that cannot be uttered except in an enigma.
This enigma is not a verbal riddle but the existential mystery of
life itself." (72-73)

"The importance of this Zen intuition of reality is, in my
opinion as a Catholic, its metaphysical honesty. It refuses to
make a claim to any special revelation or to a mystical light,
and yet if it is followed on, in line with its own vast and open
perspectives, it is certainly compatible with a revelation of
inscrutable freedom, love, and grace. In point of fact, we must
always remember that Zen is situated in the religious context of
a Buddhism which seeks the 'salvation' of all creatures by
insight. In this context, insight is extraordinarily well defined
and salvation extremely vague. In Christianity the revelation of
a salvific will and grace is simple and clear. The insight implicit
in faith, which being deepened and expanded by the mysticism
of the Fathers and of a St. John of the Cross, remains obscure

and difficult of access. It is, in fact, ignored by most Christians. Zen offers us a phenomenology and meta-physic of insight and of consciousness which has extraordinary value for the West." (254)

"Existentialism is an experience and an attitude, rather than a system of thought. As soon as it begins to present itself as a system, it denies and destroys itself. Non-objective, elusive, concrete, dynamic, always in movement and always seeking to renew itself in the newness of the present situation, genuine existentialism is, like Zen Buddhism and like apophatic Christian mysticism, hidden in life itself. It cannot be distilled out in verbal formulas. Above all, the journalistic cliches about existentialist nihilism, pessimism, anarchism, and so on, are totally irrelevant, even though they may have some foundation in certain existentialist writings. It is my contention that these writings cannot fairly be taken as representative of genuine existentialism." (258)

"True openness means the acceptance of one's own existence and one's own possibilities in confrontation with, and in free, vital relation with, the existence and potentialities of the other." (268)

"Far from being a negative cult of life- denying despair, existential theology challenges the sterility and the inner hopelessness, the spurious optimism and the real despair which masks itself in the secular and positivist illusion." (279) end Merton quotes

One must ask only a few essential questions in order to either close the theological gap between all mysticism, or cut them totally asunder from one another.
1) Do mystics sit in the presence of the same deity, consciousness, or power?
2) Do mystics reach the same state of unity or awareness?

3) Do their techniques have commonality?

Merton has shown us the parallels between Zen Buddhism and Christianity. He has shown us the commonality and shared destination of the mystical state. All mystical paths are branches of the same tree and all lead to the same root.

The answer to all three questions appears to be, "yes." By reading the thoughts and feelings of mystics from Christianity, Judaism, Buddhism, Islam, and Hindu faiths we can easily see their experiences are the same. They have the same love and joy, the same awareness and the same concept of unity with their spiritual source. As for techniques and practices of prayer and meditation, there may be outward differences but the results deliver the mystic to the same internal destination.

Zen Buddhism wishes to clear and stop the mind. Others may meditate on a single divine attribute or word until the mind is stilled and nothing exists outside the single point. Then the single point disappears and the mind itself ceases to be. In that moment we understand that we are not our body or mind, but we exist beyond both, in the eternal present, with life and being flowing through us, emanating the love that sustains us.

Zen and Buddhism

Zen is a form of Buddhism.
Buddhism is a religion or philosophy that encompasses a variety of traditions, beliefs and spiritual practices largely based on teachings attributed to Gautama Buddha, commonly known as the Buddha ("the awakened one").

According to Buddhist tradition, the Buddha lived and taught in the northeastern part of the Indian subcontinent sometime between the 6th and 4th centuries BCE.

He is recognized by Buddhists as an awakened or enlightened teacher who shared his insights to help sentient beings end their suffering through the elimination of ignorance and desire or craving. Buddhists believe that this is accomplished through direct understanding and the perception of dependent origination and the Four Noble Truths.

The Truth of Dukkha (suffering) is that all conditional phenomena and experiences are not ultimately satisfying;

The Truth of the Origin of Dukkha is that craving for and clinging to what is pleasurable and aversion to what is not pleasurable result in becoming, rebirth, dissatisfaction, and redeath;

The Truth of the Cessation of Dukkha is that putting an end to this craving and clinging also means that rebirth, dissatisfaction, and redeath can no longer arise;

The Truth of the Path Of Liberation from Dukkha (suffering) is that by following the Noble Eightfold Path—namely, behaving decently, cultivating discipline, and practicing mindfulness and meditation—an end can be put to craving, to clinging, to becoming, to rebirth, to dissatisfaction, and to redeath.

Two major extant branches of Buddhism are generally recognized by scholars: Theravada ("The School of the Elders") and Mahayana ("The Great Vehicle"). Theravada has a widespread following in Sri Lanka and Southeast Asia, while Mahayana is found throughout the Himalaya region and East Asia. In Theravada Buddhism, the ultimate goal is the attainment of the sublime state of Nirvana, by practicing the Noble Eightfold Path (also known as the Middle Way), thus escaping what is seen as a cycle of suffering and rebirth.

Right view
Right intention
Right speech
Right action
Right livelihood
Right effort
Right mindfulness
Right concentration

Mahayana Buddhism instead aspires to Buddhahood via the bodhisattva path, a state wherein one remains in this cycle to help other beings reach awakening. Vajrayana, a body of teachings attributed to Indian siddhas, may be viewed as a third branch or merely a part of Mahayana.

Tibetan Buddhism preserves the Vajrayana teachings of eighth century India. Tibetan Buddhism aspires to Buddhahood or rainbow body.

The journey for an ascetic or monk would be as follows:

Dhammalsaddhalpabbajja: A layman hears a Buddha teach the Dhamma, comes to have faith in him, and decides to take ordination as a monk;

Sila: He adopts the moral precepts;

Indriyasamvara: He practises "guarding the six sense-doors";

Sati-sampajanna: He practises mindfulness and self-possession (actually described as mindfulness of the body, kdydnussati);

Jhana 1: He finds an isolated spot in which to meditate, purifies his mind of the hindrances (nwarana), and attains the first rupa-jhana; (jhana – mental stillness and concentration)
Jhana 2: He attains the second jhana';
Jhana 3: He attains the third jhana;
Jhana 4: He attains the fourth jhana;

Pubbenivasanussati-nana: he recollects his many former existences in samsara;

Sattanam cutupapata-nana: he observes the death and rebirth of beings according to their karmas;

Dsavakkhaya-nana: He brings about the destruction of the dsavas (cankers), and attains a profound realization of (as opposed to mere knowledge about) the four noble truths;

Vimutti: He perceives that he is now liberated, that he has done what was to be done.

Buddhist schools vary on the exact nature of the path to liberation, the importance and canonicity of various teachings and scriptures, and especially their respective practices.

Buddhists do not believe in "God" in traditional sense. Gautama Buddha rejected the existence of a creator deity and did not endorse any view on creation. He stated that questions on the origin of the world are not ultimately useful for ending suffering. In Buddhism, the sole aim of spiritual practice is the complete alleviation of suffering. This state of "no-suffering" is called Nirvana.

However, describing Buddhism as nontheistic may be overly simplistic. Buddhists consider veneration of those who have attained Nirvana and the Three Jewels (Buddha, his teachings, and the Buddhist community of monks and nuns) very important. While Theravada Buddhists view the Buddha as a human being who attained Buddhahood through human efforts, some Mahayana Buddhists consider him an embodiment of the cosmic dharmakāya (truth body, formless body), born for the benefit of others. In addition, some Mahayana Buddhists worship Avalokiteśvara and hope to embody him, who constitutes the unmanifested, "inconceivable" (acintya) aspect of a Buddha, out of which Buddhas arise and to which they return after their dissolution. Buddhas are manifestations of the transformation body.

Reginald Ray writes of it as "the body of reality itself, without specific, delimited form, wherein the Buddha is identified with the spiritually charged nature of everything that is."

Some Buddhists accept the existence of beings in higher realms known as devas, but they, like humans, are suffering and are no wiser than humans. In fact, the Buddha is said to be the teacher of the gods, and he is thus superior to them. Because devas are viewed on the same level as humans there are enlightened devas, just as there are enlightened men and women.

Some sects of Buddhism believe in an "Eternal Buddha", which is a representation of omnipresent enlightenment and a symbol of the true nature of the universe. Compare this idea to the Christian idea of the mind of Christ or the Christ nature.

Philippians 2:5-11 King James Version (KJV)
5 Let this mind be in you, which was also in Christ Jesus:
6 Who, being in the form of God, thought it not robbery to be equal with God:
7 But made himself of no reputation, and took upon him the form of a servant, and was made in the likeness of men...

Finally, even though most Buddhists are considered to be "non-theists" there is the belief that enlightenment allows one to transcend, see their connection to the all, universal love, or similar concepts. Buddhists resist naming this love or light, or "Eternal Buddha" God since it limits the concept and brings up the ideas of fear and control, which goes against the aim of freedom from suffering.

The basic philosophical force of traditional Buddhism may be seen in the "Twin Verses" spoken by Buddha.

1. All that we are is the result of what we have thought: it is founded on our thoughts, it is made up of our thoughts. If a man speaks or acts with an evil thought, pain follows him, as the wheel follows the foot of the ox that draws the carriage.

2. All that we are is the result of what we have thought: it is founded on our thoughts, it is made up of our thoughts. If a man speaks or acts with a pure thought, happiness follows him, like a shadow that never leaves him.

3. "He abused me, he beat me, he defeated me, he robbed me,"—in those who harbor such thoughts hatred will never cease.

4. "He abused me, he beat me, he defeated me, he robbed me," — in those who do not harbor such thoughts hatred will cease.

5. For hatred does not cease by hatred at any time: hatred ceases by love, this is an old rule.

6. The world does not know that we must all come to an end here; — but those who know it, their quarrels cease at once.

7. He who lives looking for pleasures only, his senses uncontrolled, immoderate in his food, idle, and weak, Mara (the tempter) will certainly overthrow him, as the wind throws down a weak tree.

8. He who lives without looking for pleasures, his senses well controlled, moderate in his food, faithful and strong, him Mara will certainly not overthrow, any more than the wind throws down a rocky mountain.

9. He who wishes to put on the yellow dress without having cleansed himself from sin, who disregards temperance and truth, is unworthy of the yellow dress.

10. But he who has cleansed himself from sin, is well grounded in all virtues, and regards also temperance and truth, he is indeed worthy of the yellow dress.

11. They who imagine truth in untruth, and see untruth in truth, never arrive at truth, but follow vain desires.

12. They who know truth in truth, and untruth in untruth, arrive at truth, and follow true desires.

13. As rain breaks through an ill-thatched house, passion will break through an unreflecting mind.

14. As rain does not break through a well-thatched house, passion will not break through a well-reflecting mind.

15. The evil-doer mourns in this world, and he mourns in the next; he mourns in both. He mourns and suffers when he sees the evil of his own work.

16. The virtuous man delights in this world, and he delights in the next; he delights in both. He delights and rejoices, when he sees the purity of his own work.

17. The evil-doer suffers in this world, and he suffers in the next; he suffers in both. He suffers when he thinks of the evil he has done; he suffers more when going on the evil path.

18. The virtuous man is happy in this world, and he is happy in the next; he is happy in both. He is happy when he thinks of the good he has done; he is still more happy when going on the good path.

19. The thoughtless man, even if he can recite a large portion (of the law), but is not a doer of it, has no share in the priesthood, but is like a cowherd counting the cows of others.

20. The follower of the law, even if he can recite only a small portion (of the law), but, having forsaken passion and hatred and foolishness, possesses true knowledge and serenity of mind, he, caring for nothing in this world or that to come, has indeed a share in the priesthood.

ZEN

Zen Buddhism is a school of Mahayana Buddhism that developed in China during the Tang dynasty as Chán. From China, Chán spread south to Vietnam, northeast to Korea and east to Japan, where it became known as Japanese Zen.

Zen emphasizes rigorous meditation-practice, insight into Buddha-nature, and the personal expression of this insight in daily life, especially for the benefit of others.

Zen favors direct understanding through meditation and interaction with an accomplished teacher.

The koans or sayings of Zen, on which the student meditates, are designed to thwart the logical mind and open the intuitive nature, which can experience the divine state of enlightenment. The logical mind cannot accept what will be experienced internally and will argue for explanations which will kill or limit the awakening.

Examples of famous koans are:

A Cup of Tea
Nan-in, a Japanese master during the Meiji era (1868-1912), received a university professor who came to inquire about Zen. Nan-in served tea. He poured his visitor's cup full, and then kept on pouring.
The professor watched the overflow until he no longer could restrain himself. "It is overfull. No more will go in!"
"Like this cup," Nan-in said, "you are full of your own opinions and speculations. How can I show you Zen unless you first empty your cup?"

One Hand Clapping

The master of Kennin temple was Mokurai, Silent Thunder. He had a little protege named Toyo who was only twelve years old. Toyo saw the older disciples visit the master's room each morning and evening to receive instruction in sanzen or personal guidance in which they were given koans to stop mind-wandering.

Toyo wished to do sanzen (meditation) also.

"Wait a while," said Mokurai. "You are too young."

But the child insisted, so the teacher finally consented.

In the evening little Toyo went at the proper time to the threshold of Mokurai's sanzen room. He struck the gong to announce his presence, bowed respectfully three times outside the door, and went to sit before the master in respectful silence.

"You can hear the sound of two hands when they clap together," said Mokurai. "Now show me the sound of one hand."

Toyo bowed and went to his room to consider this problem. From his window he could hear the music of the geishas. "Ah, I have it!" he proclaimed.

The next evening, when his teacher asked him to illustrate the sound of one hand, Toyo began to play the music of the geishas.

"No, no," said Mokurai. "That will never do. That is not the sound of one hand. You've not got it at all."

Thinking that such music might interrupt, Toyo moved his abode to a quiet place. He meditated again. "What can the sound of one hand be?" He happened to hear some water dripping. "I have it," imagined Toyo.

When he next appeared before his teacher, Toyo imitated dripping water.

"What is that?" asked Mokurai. "That is the sound of dripping water, but not the sound of one hand. Try again."

In vain Toyo meditated to hear the sound of one hand. He heard the sighing of the wind. But the sound was rejected. He heard the cry of an owl. This also was refused.

The sound of one hand was not the locusts.

For more than ten times Toyo visited Mokurai with different sounds. All were wrong. For almost a year he pondered what the sound of one hand might be.

At last little Toyo entered true meditation and transcended all sounds. "I could collect no more," he explained later, "so I reached the soundless sound."

Toyo had realized the sound of one hand.

Possible, the best known Koan, and the one that has inspired books is:

If you meet the Buddha on the road, kill him.

The road is the path to Enlightenment that might be through meditation, study, prayer, or some aspect of your way of life. Your life is your road. But how do you meet the Buddha on this "road?"

Would he be a great teacher that you might actually meet and follow in the real world? Could Buddha be you yourself, having reached Enlightenment? Or maybe you have some image or concept of the Buddha or Enlightenment.

Whatever your conception is of the Buddha, it's wrong. How could you know what it is when you have not experienced it? Kill that image and keep practicing. Reality is an impermanent illusion that changes each time information, impressions, and perspectives change. If you believe that you have a correct image of what it means to be Enlightened, then you need to kill that image and keep walking the path.

As the Tao Te Ching says: "The Tao that can be named is not the eternal Tao."

Koans may guide the meditation by shutting down the mind, but the goal is to transcend the koan.

(From "The Zennist" publication)
"Zen is a mystical form of Buddhism. When Zen came to the West it came to a world-view deeply entrenched in various materialistic philosophies such as phenomenalism which believes there is nothing beyond sensory experience. Under such a view, Westerners were not eager to embrace an Asian religion which was oriented towards mysticism; which professed to transcend sensory experience and realize a transcendent experience. What they wanted was a religion that helped them cope with being a cog is the machinery of materialism. With a little tweaking, Zen became the perfect answer. It was marketed by Western Zen teachers as the antidote for our daily neurosis. This representation of Zen believed that the stresses in our lives were caused by over thinking. This harkens back to a time in American history when it was believed that neurasthenia (i.e., neurosis) was understood to be caused by "excessive brain work". In the 20th century remake of this, Zen became the practice of nonthinking as a way to cope with stress. Nonthinking, in which excessive brain work is diminished, is achieved, according to Dainin Katagiri, when we "think not-thinking"! Of course,this in itself in not in accord with the traditional Zen practice.

Despite the fact the history of Zen knew nothing of nonthinking as an antidote for neurosis or as a way to achieve enlightenment, such a belief, nevertheless, remains embedded in the circles of Western Zen. Yet, the bulk of classical Zen literature says essentially nothing about the suppression of thoughts. In fact, it says the opposite. According to the Zen master Hui-neng, non-thinking just means not to be carried away by our thoughts in the process of thinking. More importantly, we should know and see, as a mystical experience, the very medium of thought, itself, which is pure and radiant. As a consequence of knowing and seeing this pure medium, when a thought arises and then stops we know, intrinsically, the medium remains selfsame; which is our true nature. This is what Hui-neng really means by not getting carried away."

According to the book, "A History of Zen Buddhism": "Buddhism seeks to give rise to a mystical experience in which the practitioner transcends their previous state and thus it must be regarded as a religion. Buddha, and those who followed him saw in mystical enlightenment the 'vehicle of salvation' that carried them beyond this world to the 'other shore'"

Transcendence gives rise to the mystical experience in which the truth about striving, desire, and suffering is revealed. This provides deliverance from suffering. Deliverance from the human condition of desire and suffering is salvation.

The chatter of the mind and the trap of desire and suffering hold us fast within the illusion. To reach the point where the mind is quiet enough that the truth may be seen, seekers are taught to be mindful of all activities, each step, each breath, each task, as a way of suppressing troubling thoughts.

The mystical experience occurs when the process of quieting the mind allows us to transcendentally detach from our condition and we experience a clear distinction between the body to which we are seemingly bound, and our eternal nature, which is free and independent.

When we accept our state of embodiment we fall prey to attachment to our body and existence, leading to suffering. We imprison our awareness and our mental life is the cause of embodiment. One might say that we fall from our transcendental state and trap ourselves by our desire for the body and the world it has carved out for itself.

By turning our awareness to what in Buddhism is called the undying-element we experience a separation from our previous embodied condition. This is Nirvana.

In Nirvana, one is spiritually separate from the body and we realize the body is one thing and I – the real me – is not the body. It is like a vehicle, a puppet, which I animate, use and move, but I have no real connection with it. I am independent of it.

Because up to this point we know only our sensory input from our body so we have no way to accurately describe the spiritual sickness that has beset us. This is because we do not know how it feels to be healthy. This mystical experience is separate from the body, we have no way of describing with any accuracy the mystical phenomena.

Traditionally, Zen has sought to experience the transcendent, which is not connected with the body. Traditional Zen is not interested in limiting meditation to sitting or to any posture. The act of daily living must become our meditation and it has to be ongoing. For Zen, meditation is an inner quest.

This is not to say that monks do not meditate. They do, but they know it is not necessary. They remain detached from the process. They know it is simply one means to an end.

"The Zennist" publication reports:
"This is what is expressed in the first print of Kaku-an's remarkable Ten Ox Herding Prints. The Zennist, as a young oxherd, is depicted as searching for his lost ox. In D.T. Suzuki's translation of the commentary to the first ox herding print, the ox is a metaphor for our true nature which we have lost sight of. The reason that the ox is lost is because of our deluding senses which aspire to worldly gain. The first stanza goes: "Alone in the wilderness, lost in the jungle, the boy is searching, searching!" It goes without saying, that this is a meditative search for our transcendent nature—not our mundane psychological nature which confronts the rat race."

Without a commitment to the transcendent experience and the mystical process no progress can be made. Yet, in a way, attachment to this process will stall the process completely. There can be no attachment to hold us here. Not even the process that may release us.

The ultimate standpoint of Zen is that we have been led astray through ignorance to find a split in our own being, that there was from the very beginning no need for a struggle between the finite and the infinite, that the peace we are seeking so eagerly after has been there all the time.
D.T. Suzuki

The following are Zen sayings, which may lead us to a deeper understanding of the mystical path found in this "religion".

Sitting Quietly
Sitting quietly, doing nothing,
Spring comes, and the grass grows by itself.
(The Way of Zen 134, 222)

Suchness
The blue mountains are of themselves blue mountains;
The white clouds are of themselves white clouds.
 (The Way of Zen 134, 222)

Mountains are Mountains
Before I had studied Zen for thirty years, I saw mountains as mountains, and waters as waters. When I arrived at a more intimate knowledge, I came to the point where I saw that mountains are not mountains, and waters are not waters. But now that I have got its very substance I am at rest. For it's just that I see mountains once again as mountains, and waters once again as waters.
(The Way of Zen 220 k)

Eternity in an hour
An eternity of endless space:
A day of wind and moon.
(The Golden Age of Zen 246, 322 n.2)

The Root
Nan-ch'uan and his lay disciple Lu Hsuan. Lu was reciting
Seng-chao's saying:
Heaven and earth come from the same root as myself:
All things and I belong to one Whole.
However, he did not really understand the full purport of it.
Nan-ch'uan pointed at the peonies in the courtyard, saying,
'The worldlings look at these bush of flowers as in a dream. Lu
did not see the point. (The Golden Age of Zen 285)

Merge your mind with cosmic space, integrate your actions
with myriad forms.
Ch'an master Hung-chih Cheng-chüeh Wanshi Shōkaku, 1091-
1157)

Entering the forest he moves not the grass;
Entering the water he makes not a ripple.
Zenrin Kushû (The Way of Zen 152, 224)

Everyday Mind
There's nothing equal to wearing clothes and eating food.
Outside this there are neither Buddhas nor Patriarchs.
Zenrin Kushû (The Way of Zen 152, 224)

Seeking the Same Thing
From the K'un-lun mountains eastward the (Taoist) term "Great
Oneness" is used. From Kashmir westward the (Buddhist) term
sambodhi (enlightenment – awakening) is used. Whether one
looks longingly toward "non-being" (wu) or cultivates
"emptiness" (sunyata), the principle involved is the same.

(The Way of Zen 82)

Ocean of Pure Reality
Ocean of pure Reality,
Its substance, in fathomless quiescence, exists eternally.
Ch'an master Fo-kuang Ju-man (Bukkõ Nyoman)

Great Unity
There is one thing: above, it supports Heaven; below, it
upholds Earth. It is black like lacquer, always actively
functioning.
Ch'an master Tung-shan Ling-chia (Tõsan Ryõkai, 807-869)

Man of Tao (Man of the Way)
Like the clear stillness of autumn water — pure and without
activity; in its tranquil depths are no obstructions. Such a one is
called a man of Tao, also, a man who has nothing further to do.
Wei-shan Ling-yu (Isan Reiyû)

Nondiscrimination
When you forget the good and the non-good, the worldly life
and the religious life, and all other dharmas, and permit no
thoughts relating to them to arise, and you abandon body and
mind — then there is complete freedom. When the mind is like
wood or stone, there is nothing to be discriminated.
Pai-chang Huai-hai (Hyakujõ Ekai, 720-814)

Speech and Silence
Speech is blasphemy, silence a lie. Above speech and silence
there is a way out.
(The Golden Age of Zen 250, 322 n.13)

Inexpressible
What is inexpressible is inexhaustible in its use.
A Chinese Zen master (The Golden Age of Zen 253, 322 n.19)

Independent
I would rather sink to the bottom of the sea for endless eons
than seek liberation through all the saints of the universe.
Shih-t'ou (The Golden Age of Zen 270, 323 n.57)

Individual
The full-grown man aspires to pierce through the heavens:
Let him not walk in the footsteps of the Buddha!
Ts'ui-yen (The Golden Age of Zen 270, 323 n.59)

No Words
No dependence upon words and letters;
Direct pointing at the soul of man;
Seeing into one's nature and the attainment of Buddhahood.

Accomplishing Beforehand
When the task is done beforehand, then it is easy.
Zen master Yuan-tong
(The Tao of Abundance 100)

Begin at the Top
If you want to climb a mountain, begin at the top.
Zen saying

Every Day is a Good Day
Everyday is a good day.
No Work, No Eating
A day without work, a day without eating.

Living Dead
At the funeral of one of his monks, as the Abbot joined the
procession, he remarked, 'What a long procession of dead
bodies follows the wake of a single living person!'
(The Golden Age of Zen 145, 309 n.47)

Mind is Buddha
Asked "What is buddha?" Ma-tsu replied "This very mind, this is Buddha."
Asked "What is buddha?" Ma-tsu replied "Neither mind nor Buddha."
"This is not mind, this is not Buddha, this is not a thing."
(The Development of Chinese Zen After the Sixth Patriarch 55)

No Clinging
No clinging, no seeking.
(The Development of Chinese Zen After the Sixth Patriarch 62)

Dharma
All Dharmas are Mind-Created
Therefore the Three Realms are only mind
(The Development of Chinese Zen After the Sixth Patriarch 54)

(Dharma has no direct word of translation into English. The word has been rendered as: that which is established or firm, steadfast decree, statute, law, practice, custom, duty, right, justice, virtue, morality, ethics, religion, religious merit, good works, nature, character, quality, property, right way of living and path of righteousness.)

Reality
Ultimate reality has a unified form. Buddha.
(Early Ch'an in China and Tibet 107)

No Delusive Thoughts
Away with your delusive thoughts! Don't be deluded!
Ch'an master Wu-ye (Mugō, 760-821) (Zen Word, Zen Calligraphy 65)

Who - What
Whatever the master was asked, he replied "Maku mōzō!"
Who is This
I know not.

Bodhidharma

No Merit At All
Vast emptiness, nothing holy!
Bodhidharma

Drop
Body and mind dropped away.
Casting off both body and mind.
(Zen Master Dogen 32)

No Thought
No though, no cultivation, no intention. Let it settle itself.
Tao Te Ching

Abide Nowhere
When the two were face to face in the stillness of the night, the
Patriarch expounded the Diamond Sutra to his disciple. When
he came to the sentence: "Keep your mind alive and free
without abiding in anything or anywhere, Hui-neng was
suddenly and thoroughly enlightened"
(The Golden Age of Zen 62)

Holding fast to nothing is not the same as not holding fast to
anything. The very idea of nothing must also disappear. The
mind must become as still as a stone and as peaceful as a
windless pond. When all things are forgotten and buried
beneath the cloud of Un-knowing and the mind is empty, that
is where the Zen and Christian mystics meet.

Zen has to do with becoming as a little child. Unless we
become little children we cannot enter "the kingdom." Live in
awe, with a free and clear mind, having no preconceived ideas.
Be totally focused on each moment. Do things as if it were your
first time each time. Do things as if it was your last act.
Completely aware – everywhere – all the time. The wonder!

Islam and its Mystics

Islam, like Christianity and Judaism, is a monotheistic, Abrahamic religion originating in the Middle East.

The rise of Islam is intrinsically linked with the Prophet Muhammad, believed by Muslims to be the last in a long line of prophets that includes Moses and Jesus. Because Muhammad was the chosen recipient and messenger of the word of God through the divine revelations, Muslims from all walks of life strive to follow his example.

Muhammad was born into the most powerful tribe in Mecca, the Quraish, around 570 CE. The power of the Quraish derived from their role as successful merchants. Several trade routes intersected at Mecca, allowing the Quraish to control trade along the west coast of Arabia, north to Syria, and south to Yemen.

Mecca was home to two widely venerated polytheistic cults whose gods were thought to protect its lucrative trade.

When he was approximately forty years of age, Muhammad began having visions and hearing voices. Searching for clarity, he would sometimes meditate at Mount Hira, near Mecca. On one of these occasions, the Archangel Gabriel (Jibra'il in Arabic) appeared to him and instructed him to recite "in the name of [your] lord." This was the first of many revelations that became the basis of the Qur'an, the holy book of Islam.

These early revelations pointed to the existence of a single God, contradicting the polytheistic beliefs of the pre-Islamic Arabian Peninsula. At this point in time there were few monotheists.

Judaism and Christianity predate Islam and were there but polytheism still held sway.

Muhammad's strong monotheistic message angered many of the Meccan merchants. They were afraid that trade, which they believed was protected by the pagan gods, would suffer. From that point forward, Muhammad was ostracized and ejected from Mecca.

Escape became the only hope for Muhammad and his followers' survival. In 622 CE, they ran to Medina, another oasis town, where they were promised freedom to practice their religion. The move from Mecca to Medina is known as the hijra — the flight — and marks year 1 of the Islamic, or hijri, calendar.

In Medina, Muhammad continued to receive divine revelations. It was at this point that Muhammad began to change Islam from a religion of peace and acceptance to one of actively converting unbelievers.

Islam is articulated by the Qur'an, a religious text considered by its adherents to be the verbatim word of God (Allāh) as Allah dictated it to the prophet, Muhammad (c. 570–8 June 632 CE). However, the history of Muhammad and his teachings indicate he began the religion as a teacher of peace but ended as a warrior.

The Qur'an is interpreted as an unfolding revelation in which the last word or command of the prophet supersedes all prior viewpoints and commands. This is one reason fundamental Muslims believe non-believers should be killed.

Muslims believe that God is one and incomparable and that the purpose of existence is to worship God. Muslims also believe that Islam is the complete and universal version of a primordial faith that was revealed many times before through prophets including Adam, Noah, Abraham, Moses, and Jesus.

They maintain that the previous messages and revelations have been partially misinterpreted or altered over time, but consider the Arabic Qur'an to be both the unaltered and the final revelation of God.

The practice of Islam is based on the five pillars. The Pillars of Islam are five basic acts in Islam, considered obligatory for all believers. The Quran presents them as a framework for worship and a sign of commitment to the faith.
They are:
(1) the creed (shahadah),
(2) daily prayers (salat),
(3) almsgiving (zakah),
(4) fasting during Ramadan and
(5) the pilgrimage to Mecca (hajj) at least once in a lifetime.

Both Shia and Sunni sects agree on the essential details for the performance of these acts.

Most Muslims are of two denominations: Sunni (75–90%) or Shia (10–20%). Converts and immigrant communities are found in almost every part of the world. With about 1.62 billion followers or 23% of the global population, Islam is the second-largest religion by number of adherents and, according to many sources, the fastest-growing major religion in the world

The mystics of Islam tend to interpret the prophet's teachings regarding war and killing in a metaphorical sense based on the teaching, "Jihad al-Akbar, The Greatest Jihad: Combat with the Self." This sums up the internal struggle and the importance of purifying the soul.

"Jihad is of three kinds; the carrying out of a struggle against:
1. a visible enemy,

2. the devil,
3. one's self."

The greatest Jihad is the war within.

Thus, in a broader sense, jihad means striving to the utmost
extent of one's ability and power by exerting oneself spiritually
in the way of Allah and doing one's best to preach the message
of Islam to others. Muslims will choose which jihad to pursue
and by what path they accomplish their mission and these
choices determine if they will be a mystic or a terrorist.

**The jihad referred to here is clearly jihad bil nafs -- the
spiritual exertion to curb one's lower desires and evil
inclinations and to try to increase in the doing of good in
order to attain nearness to Allah. This form of jihad against
one's own self is perhaps the most difficult of all. A believer
sincerely tries to purify his soul and asks help from his
Creator, he finds Him nigh and God guides him in his
efforts. This is the Sufi way.**

Sufism is the mystical arm of Islam, Sufism is a selfless
experiencing and actualization of the Truth. The practice of
Sufism is the intention to go towards the Truth, by means of
love and devotion. This is called the *tarigat*, the spiritual path or
way towards God. The Sufi is one who is a lover of Truth, who
by means of love and devotion moves towards the Truth,
towards the perfection which all are truly seeking. As
necessitated by love's jealousy, the Sufi is taken away from all
except the Truth. Sufism is a school for the actualization of
divine ethics. It involves an enlightened inner being, not
intellectual proof; revelation and witnessing, not logic. By
divine ethics, we are referring to ethics that transcend mere
social convention, a way of being that is the actualization of the
attributes of God.

Revelation, witnessing, experiencing the pure truth, this is the way of all mystics.

There are sects of off-shoots of the Sufi way. Another arm of mysticism in the Muslim faith is the Dervish. A dervish or darvesh is someone treading a Sufi Muslim ascetic path or "Tariqah", known for their extreme poverty and austerity. Many become beggars in order to learn humility. His focus is on the universal values of love and service deserting the illusions of ego to reach God. In most Sufi orders, a dervish is known to practice dhikr through physical exertions or religious practices to attain ecstatic trance to reach Allah.

The whirling dance of the Dervish is proverbially associated with the Mevlevi order in Turkey, and is part of a formal ceremony known as the Sema. It is, however, also practiced by other orders. The Sema is only one of the many Sufi ceremonies performed to try to reach religious ecstasy. The name Mevlevi comes from the Persian poet Rumi, who was a Dervish himself. Whatever the differences in the Sufi way, all Sufis seek, not only the truth, but a direct connection to the truth and Allah.

To explain the Truth is indeed a difficult task. Words, being limited, can never really express the perfection of the Absolute, the Unbound. Thus, for those who are imperfect, words create doubt and misunderstanding. Yet:

If one cannot drink up the entire ocean,
    one can drink to one's limit.

Philosophers have written volumes and spoken endlessly of the Truth, but somehow their efforts have always fallen short. For the Sufi, philosophers are those who view the Perfection of the Absolute from a limited perspective; so all they see is part of the Absolute, not the Infinite in its entirety. It is indeed true that what philosophers see is correct; nevertheless, it is only a part of the whole.

One is reminded of Rumi's well-known story of a group of men in India who had never seen an elephant. One day they came to a place where an elephant was. In complete darkness they approached the animal, each man feeling it. Afterwards, they described what they thought they had perceived. Of course their descriptions were different. The one who felt a leg, imagined the elephant to be a pillar. The one who felt the animal's ear, described the elephant as a fan, and so on. Each one of their descriptions with respect to the various parts they had experienced was true. However, as far as accurately describing the whole, their conceptions had all fallen short. If they had had a candle, the difference of opinions would not have come about. The candle's light would have revealed the elephant as a whole.

Only by the light of the Spiritual Path and the mystic way can the Truth be discovered. In order for one to truly witness the Perfection of the Absolute Truth, one must see with one's inner being, which perceives the whole of Reality. This witnessing happens when one becomes perfect, losing one's (partial) existence in the Whole. If the Whole is likened to the Ocean, and the part to a drop, the Sufi says that witnessing the Ocean with the eye of a drop is impossible. However, when the drop becomes one with the Ocean, it sees the Ocean with the eye of the Ocean.

The stages of purification are:
1. self becoming emptied
2. self becoming illuminated
3. self becoming adorned
4. self having passed away

(The similarities of these four steps to those of Zen Buddhism and the Christian "Cloud of Un-knowing" is stunning.)

These stages occur in the course of the selfless remembrance of God (dhikr). The first stage, becoming emptied, entails letting go of negative qualities, the desires which originate from the self. The second stage of becoming illuminated involves polishing the heart and soul of the tarnish of belief in and attachment to the self. In the third stage, one's inner being becomes adorned by Divine Attributes. Ultimately, the being of the disciple becomes completely filled by the Attributes of the Truth, to the extent that there is no sign of his own limited existence. This fourth stage is called "self-having passed-away" (fana).

People pray in order to draw God's compassion and grace upon themselves. In their prayers, they beg God to bestow His benevolence upon them and not His wrath. But the Sufi is one who is in love with the Beloved. Whether the Beloved is clothed in the garb of benevolence or wrath makes no difference. How, then, can the Sufi pray for anything, when all he or she sees is the Beloved and not the outer garment?

This is what Paul meant when he said, "Pray without ceasing." It is not about words. It is about relationship to and in God. It is a state of love and gratitude toward God.

One who prays to God for something prays from a 'self'. Such beseeching becomes a manifestation of an individual consciousness before Absolute Being. However, the enraptured lover cannot at all be conscious of his or her own existence before the Absolute, as that would be infidelity to the Beloved.

Bayazid has said: "From the time of initiation into love, I have been ashamed to ask anything from God, but God himself. Even to my daily prayers, required by religion, I always added, "Oh God, you know what Bayazid wants!"

This reflects the words of David when he said, "What can I give God for all He has done for me? I can only lift the cup of my deliverance and call upon His name."

In the words of Rumi: I know a group of saints; 'their' mouths are shut to prayer.

Since the Sufis want only what God wants, and have no 'self' from which to pray, how can they pray for anything? Indeed, how can 'they' pray at all?

Thus, when the Sufi prays, 'he' or 'she' is not praying and consequently cannot pray for anything.

There is disagreement among religious scholars and Sufis themselves about the origins of Sufism. The traditional view is that Sufism is the mystical school of Islam and had its beginnings in the first centuries following the life of the Prophet Mohammad. Indeed, most Sufis in the world today are Muslim and many of them would consider a non-Islamic Sufism impossible.

There is another view, however, that traces the pre-Islamic roots of Sufism back through the early Christian mystics of Syria and Egypt, to the Essenes, the ancient Pythagorean orders, and the mystery schools of the Egyptians and Zoroastrians, among others. It is these roots that gathered into the trunk known as Islamic Sufism.

Sufi Inayat Khan recognized the multi-religious roots of Sufism as well as its contemporary relevance for people of all faiths. When he was instructed by his teacher in 1907 to bring Sufism to the West, he articulated a "message of spiritual liberty" which reflects the universal, inclusive nature of Sufism. As he noted:

Every age of the world has seen awakened souls, and as it is impossible to limit wisdom to any one period or place, so it is impossible to date the origin of Sufism.
Texts on the Universality of Sufism

The Origin of Sufism - Sufi Inayat Khan:
The germ of Sufism is said to have existed from the beginning of the human creation, for wisdom is the heritage of all; therefore no one person can be said to be its propounder. It has been revealed more clearly and spread more widely from time to time as the world has evolved.

Sufism as a brotherhood/sisterhood may be traced back as far as the period of Daniel. We find among the Zoroastrians, Hatim, the best known Sufi of his time. The chosen ones of God, the salt of the earth, who responded without hesitation to the call of Abraham, Moses, Jesus and Mohammed, were Sufis, and were not only simple followers of a religion but had insight into divine knowledge. They recognized God's every messenger and united with them all. Before the time of Mohammed they were called Ekuanul Safa, Brothers of Purity, but after his coming they were named by him Sahabi Safa, Knights of Purity. The world has called them Zoroastrian, Christian, Jewish, or Islamic mystics, and the followers of each religion have claimed them as their own. For instance, a Christian would claim that Saint Paul was a Christian and a Muslim that Shams Tabriz was a Muslim. In reality Christ was not a Christian nor was Mohammed a Muslim, they were Sufis. Sufis view all mystics as Sufis.

Sufism: Wisdom Of All Faiths - Sufi Inayat Khan:
The word Sufi comes from a Persian word meaning wisdom. From the original root many derivations can be traced; among them the Greek word Sophia is one of the most interesting.

Wisdom is the ultimate power, which leads to truth, and truth is universal. Simple followers of a religion see only their differences. The wise, whatever their faith, have always been able to meet each other beyond those boundaries of external forms and conventions, which are natural and necessary to human life, but which nonetheless separate humanity.

People of the same thought and point of view are drawn to each other with a tendency to form an exclusive circle. A minority is apt to fence itself off from the crowd. So it has been with the mystics. Mystical ideas are unintelligible to the generality of people. The mystics have, therefore, usually imparted their ideas to a chosen few, only to those whom they could trust, who were ready for initiation and discipleship. Thus great Sufis have appeared at different times and have founded schools of thought. Their expression of wisdom has differed to suit their environments, but their understanding of life has been one and the same.

Every age of the world has seen awakened souls, and as it is impossible to limit wisdom to any one period or place, so it is impossible to date the origin of Sufism. If mysticism is the same throughout the world, then mysticism predates mankind, for even the angels communed with God.

Not only have there been illuminated souls at all times, but there have been times when a wave of illumination has passed over humanity and it takes away the boundaries which divide different faiths by bringing into full light the underlying wisdom in which they are all united. The greatest of these periods was called, "The Axial Age" and now we await impatiently the coming of the Second Axial Age of enlightenment, which will be a setting aside of religion en mass in favor of a personal mystical path.

The Unity of Knowledge - Idries Shah:

The connection between the ancient practical philosophies and the present ones is seen to have been based upon the higher-level unity of knowledge, not upon appearances. This explains why the Muslim Rumi has Christian, Zoroastrian and other disciples; why the great Sufi 'invisible teacher' Khidr is said to be a Jew; why the Mogul Prince Dara Shikoh identified Sufi teachings in the Hindu Vedas, yet himself remained a member of the Qadiri Order; how Pythagoras and Solomon can be said to be Sufi teachers. It also explains why Sufis will accept some alchemists to have been Sufis, as well as understanding the underlying developmental factors in Rumi's evolutionary philosophy, or Hallaj's 'Christianity'; why, indeed, Jesus is said to stand, in a sense, at the head of the Sufis.

Origins and Nature of the Sufis - Robert Graves
(from his introduction to Idries Shah's "The Sufis"):
The Sufis are an ancient spiritual freemasonry whose origins have never been traced or dated; nor do they themselves take much interest in such researches, being content to point out the occurrence of their own way of thought in different regions and periods. Though commonly mistaken for a Moslem sect, the Sufis are at home in all religions: just as the "Free and Accepted Masons" lay before them in their Lodge whatever sacred book—whether Bible, Koran, or Torah—is accepted by the temporal State. If they call Islam the "shell" of Sufism, this is because they believe Sufism to be the secret teaching within all religions. Yet according to Ali el-Hujwiri, an early authoritative Sufi writer, the Prophet Mohammed himself said: "He who hears the voice of the Sufi people and does not say aamin [Amen] is recorded in God's presence as one of the heedless." Numerous other traditions link him with the Sufis, and it was in Sufi style that he ordered his followers to respect all People of the Book, meaning those who respected their own sacred scriptures—a term later taken to include Zoroastrians.

Nor are the Sufis a sect, being bound by no religious dogma however tenuous and using no regular place of worship. They have no sacred city, no monastic organization, no religious instruments. They even dislike being given any inclusive name which might force them into doctrinal conformity. "Sufi" is no more than a nickname, like "Quaker," which they accept good-humoredly. "We friends" or "people like us" is how they refer to themselves, and they recognize one another by certain natural gifts, habits, qualities of thought. Sufi schools have indeed gathered around particular teachers, but there is no graduation and they exist only for the convenience of those who work to perfect their studies by close association with fellow Sufis. The characteristic Sufi signature is found in widely dispersed literature from at least the second millennium BCE, and although their most obvious impact on civilization was made between the eighth and eighteenth centuries CE, Sufis are still active as ever. They number some fifty million. What makes them so difficult to discuss is that their mutual recognition cannot be explained in ordinary moral or psychological terms — whoever understands it is himself a Sufi. Though awareness of this secret quality or instinct can be sharpened by close contact with Sufis of experience, there are no hierarchical degrees among them, only a general undisputed recognition of greater or lesser capacity.

Sufism has gained an Oriental flavor from having been so long protected by Islam, but the natural Sufi may be as common in the West as in the East, and may come dressed as a general, a peasant, a merchant, a lawyer, a schoolmaster, a housewife, anything. To be "in the world, but not of it," free from ambition, greed, intellectual pride, blind obedience to custom, or awe of persons higher in rank — that is the Sufi's ideal.

Sufis respect the rituals of religion insofar as these further social harmony, but broaden religion's doctrinal basis wherever possible and define its myths in a higher sense — for instance, explaining angels as representations of man's higher faculties. The individual is offered a "secret garden" for the growth of his understanding, but never required to become a

monk, nun or hermit, like the more conventional mystics; and he thereafter claims to be enlightened by actual experience — "he who tastes, knows" — not by philosophic argument. The earliest known theory of conscious evolution is of Sufi origin...
  If we have experiences we are not at the mercy of doctrine or argument.

  (Exploring the poetry of the Sufi mystics was an enlightening but frustrating task. The body of work is overwhelming. As it became obvious that no one book could hold it all it fell on me to select works that represented the best of the huge corpus available. I could not decide what to cull, seeing as any poem could speak to a number of souls and possibly bring about insight into the depth and beauty of Sufism and their passionate search for oneness with God. I finally settled on the works of Rumi and Hafiz. Even this limited sample is large and may seem to go beyond what is needed.)

Only Breath - Jelaluddin Rumi
(translated by Coleman Barks):

Not Christian or Jew or Muslim, not Hindu
Buddhist, Sufi, or Zen. Not any religion
or cultural system. I am not from the East
or the West, not out of the ocean or up
from the ground, not natural or ethereal, not
composed of elements at all. I do not exist,
am not an entity in this world or the next,
did not descend from Adam and Eve or any
origin story. My place is placeless, a trace
of the traceless. Neither body or soul.
I belong to the beloved, have seen the two
worlds as one and that one call to and know, ·
first, last, outer, inner, only that
breath breathing human being.

136

Garden Among the Flames - Ibn 'Arabi
(translated by Michael Sells):

Wonder,
A garden among the flames!
My heart can take on
Any form:
A meadow for gazelles,
A cloister for monks,
For the idols, sacred ground,
Ka'ba for the circling pilgrim,
the tables for the Torah,
the scrolls of the Qur'an.
My creed is love;
Wherever its caravan turns along the way,
That is my belief,
My faith.

The following are poems of Rumi and reveal the depth and
expanse of the Sufi mystics:

Like grapes, we have always accompanied the vat.
From the view of the world, we have disappeared.
For years, we boiled from the fire of love
Until we became that wine, which intoxicates the world.
There is a community of the spirit.
Join it, and feel the delight
of walking in the noisy street
and being the noise.
Drink all your passion,
and be a disgrace.
Close both eyes
to see with the other eye.

Essential Rumi
by Coleman Barks
This We Have Now:

This we have now
is not imagination.
This is not
grief or joy.
Not a judging state,
or an elation,
or sadness.
Those come and go.
This is the presence that doesn't.
There is a way between voice and presence
where information flows.
In disciplined silence it opens.
With wandering talk it closes.

Moving Water:

When you do things from your soul, you feel a river
moving in you, a joy.
When actions come from another section, the feeling
disappears. Don't let others lead you. They may be blind or,
worse, vultures.
Reach for the rope of God. And what is that? Putting aside
self-will.
Because of willfulness people sit in jail, the trapped bird's
wings are tied, fish sizzle in the skillet.

The anger of police is willfulness. You've seen a magistrate
inflict visible punishment. Now see the invisible. If you could
leave your selfishness, you would see how you've been
torturing your soul. We are born and live inside black water in
a well.

How could we know what an open field of sunlight is? Don't insist on going where you think you want to go. Ask the way to the spring. Your living pieces will form a harmony. There is a moving palace that floats in the air with balconies and clear water flowing through, infinity everywhere, yet contained under a single tent.

Out beyond ideas of wrongdoing and rightdoing, there is a field. I'll meet you there.

When the soul lies down in that grass, the world is too full to talk about.
Ideas, language, even the phrase *each other* doesn't make any sense.

Light Breeze:

As regards feeling pain, like a hand cut in battle,
consider the body a robe you wear. When you meet someone you love, do you kiss their clothes? Search out who's inside.
 Union with God is sweeter than body comforts.
We have hands and feet different from these. Sometimes in dream we see them.
That is not illusion. It's seeing truly. You do have a spirit body;
don't dread leaving the physical one.
Sometimes someone feels this truth so strongly
that he or she can live in mountain solitude totally refreshed.
 The worried, heroic doings of men and women seem weary and futile to dervishes enjoying the light breeze of spirit.

Late, by myself, in the boat of myself,
no light and no land anywhere,
cloud cover thick. I try to stay

just above the surface,
yet I'm already under
and living with the ocean.

If you want what visible reality
can give, you're an employee.
If you want the unseen world,
you're not living your truth.
Both wishes are foolish,
but you'll be forgiven for forgetting
that what you really want is
love's confusing joy.

Only Breath:

Not Christian or Jew or Muslim, not Hindu
Buddhist, Sufi, or Zen. Not any religion
or cultural system. I am not from the East
or the West, not out of the ocean or up
from the ground, not natural or ethereal, not
composed of elements at all. I do not exist,
am not an entity in this world or in the next,
did not descend from Adam and Eve or any
origin story. My place is placeless, a trace
of the traceless. Neither body or soul.

I belong to the beloved, have seen the two
worlds as one and that one call to and know,
first, last, outer, inner, only that
breath breathing human being.

Birdsong brings relief
to my longing
I'm just as ecstatic as they are,
but with nothing to say!

Please universal soul, practice
some song or something through me!

Not Intrigued With Evening:

What the material world values does
not shine the same in the truth of
the soul. You have been interested
in your shadow. Look instead directly
at the sun. What can we know by just
watching the time-and-space shapes of each other?
Someone half awake in the night sees imaginary dangers;
The morning star rises; the horizon grows
defined; people become friends in a moving caravan.
Night birds may think daybreak a kind of darkness, because
that's all they know. It's a fortunate
bird who's not intrigued with evening,
who flies in the sun we call Shams.

For awhile we lived with people, but we saw no sign in them of
the faithfulness we wanted. It's better to hide completely
within as water hides in metal, as fire hides in rock.
The breeze at dawn has secrets to tell you.
Don't go back to sleep.

You must ask for what you really want.
Don't go back to sleep.

People are going back and forth across the doorsill
where the two worlds touch.

The door is round and open.
Don't go back to sleep.

Two Friends:

A certain person came to the Friend's door
and knocked.
"Who's there?"
"It's me."
The Friend answered, "Go away. There's no place
for raw meat at this table."

The individual went wandering for a year.
Nothing but the fire of separation
can change hypocrisy and ego. The person returned
completely cooked,
walked up and down in front of the Friend's house,
gently knocked.
"Who is it?"
"You."
"Please come in, my self,
there's no place in this house for two.
The doubled end of the thread is not what goes through
the eye of the needle.
It's a single-pointed, fined-down, thread end,
not a big ego-beast with baggage."

The Dream That Must Be Interpreted:

This place is a dream.
Only a sleeper considers it real.
Then death comes like dawn,
and you wake up laughing
at what you thought was your grief.
But there's a difference with this dream.
Everything cruel and unconscious

142

done in the illusion of the present world,
all that does not fade away at the death-waking.

It stays, and it must be interpreted.
All the mean laughing,
all the quick, sexual wanting,
those torn coats of Joseph,
they change into powerful wolves
that you must face.

The retaliation that sometimes comes now,
the swift, payback hit,
is just a boy's game
to what the other will be.

You know about circumcision here.
It's full castration there!

And this groggy time we live,
this is what it's like:
                    A man goes to sleep in the town
where he has always lived, and he dreams he's living
in another town.
                    In the dream, he doesn't remember
the town he's sleeping in his bed in. He believes
the reality of the dream town.
The world is that kind of sleep.
The dust of many crumbled cities
settles over us like a forgetful doze,
but we are older than those cities.

We began as a mineral. We emerged into plant life
and into the animal state, and then into being human,
and always we have forgotten our former states,
except in early spring when we slightly recall
being green again.

That's how a young person turns toward a teacher.
 That's how a baby leans toward the breast, without knowing
the secret of its desire, yet turning instinctively.

Humankind is being led along an evolving course,
through this migration of intelligences,
and though we seem to be sleeping,
there is an inner wakefulness that directs the dream,
and that will eventually startle us back to the truth of who we
are.

The Taste of Morning:

Time's knife slides from the sheath,
as fish from where it swims.
Being closer and closer is the desire of the body.
Don't wish for union!
There's a closeness beyond that.
Why would God want a second God?
Fall in love in such a way that it frees you
from any connecting. Love is the soul's
light, the taste of morning, no me, no
we, no claim of being.
These words are the smoke the fire gives off as it
absolves its defects, as eyes in silence,
tears, face. Love cannot be said.

Shadow and Light Source Both:

How does a part of the world leave the world?
How does wetness leave water? Don't try to
put out fire by throwing on more fire! Don't

wash a wound with blood. No matter how fast
you run, your shadow keeps up. Sometimes it's
in front! Only full overhead sun diminishes
your shadow. But that shadow has been serving
you. What hurts you, blesses you. Darkness is
your candle. Your boundaries are your quest.
I could explain this, but it will break the
glass cover on your heart, and there's no
fixing that. You must have shadow and light
source both. Listen, and lay your head under
the tree of awe. When from that tree feathers
and wings sprout on you, be quieter than
a dove. Don't even open your mouth for even a coo.

Who Says Words With My Mouth?

All day I think about it, then at night I say it.
Where did I come from, and what am I supposed to be doing?
I have no idea.
My soul is from elsewhere, I'm sure of that,
and I intend to end up there.

This drunkenness began in some other tavern.
When I get back around to that place,
I'll be completely sober. Meanwhile,
I'm like a bird from another continent, sitting in this aviary.
The day is coming when I fly off,
but who is it now in my ear who hears my voice?
Who says words with my mouth?

Who looks out with my eyes? What is the soul?
I cannot stop asking.
If I could taste one sip of an answer,
I could break out of this prison for drunks.

I didn't come here of my own accord, and I can't leave that
way.
Whoever brought me here will have to take me home.

This poetry, I never know what I'm going to say.
I don't plan it.
When I'm outside the saying of it,
I get very quiet and rarely speak at all.

There is a life-force within your soul, seek that life.
There is a gem in the mountain of your body, seek that
mine.

O traveler, if you are in search of That
Don't look outside, look inside yourself and seek That.
I see so deeply within myself.
Not needing my eyes, I can see everything clearly.
Why would I want to bother my eyes again
Now that I see the world through His eyes?
There is a candle in the heart of man, waiting to be kindled.
In separation from the Friend, there is a cut waiting to be
stitched.

O, you who are ignorant of endurance and the burning
fire of love----
Love comes of its own free will, it can't be learned
in any school.

If you show patience, I'll rid you of this virtue.
If you fall asleep, I'll rub the sleep from your eyes.
If you become a mountain, I'll melt you in fire.
And if you become an ocean, I'll drink all your water.
Any soul that drank the nectar of your passion was lifted.
From that water of life he is in a state of elation.
Death came, smelled me, and sensed your fragrance instead.
From then on, death lost all hope of me.
Any lifetime that is spent without seeing the master

Is either death in disguise or a deep sleep.
The water that pollutes you is poison;
The poison that purifies you is water.
Out of your love the fire of youth will rise.
In the chest, visions of the soul will rise.
If you are going to kill me, kill me, it is alright.
When the friend kills, a new life will rise.

I am blasphemy and religion, pure and impure;
Old, young, and a small child.
If I die, don't say that he died.
Say he was dead, became alive, and was taken by the
Beloved.

This aloneness is worth more than a thousand lives.
This freedom is worth more than all the lands on earth.
To be one with the truth for just a moment,
Is worth more than the world and life itself.
In the end, the mountains of imagination were nothing
but a house.

And this grand life of mine was nothing but an excuse.
You've been hearing my story so patiently for a lifetime
Now hear this: it was nothing but a fairy tale.
How long will you think about this painful life?
How long will you think about this harmful world?
The only thing it can take from you is your body.
Don't say all this rubbish and stop thinking.
In the waters of purity, I melted like salt
Neither blasphemy, nor faith, nor conviction, nor doubt
remained.

In the center of my heart a star has appeared
And all the seven heavens have become lost in it.
Until you've found pain, you won't reach the cure

Until you've given up life, you won't unite with the supreme
soul.

Until you've found fire inside yourself, like the Friend,
You won't reach the spring of life, like Khezr.
In love, aside from sipping the wine of timelessness,
 nothing else exists.
There is no reason for living except for giving one's life.
I said, "First I know you, then I die."
He said, "For the one who knows Me, there is no dying."
You personify God's message.
You reflect the King's face.
There is nothing in the universe that you are not
Everything you want, look for it within yourself--
 you are that.

The minute I heard my first love story,
I started looking for you, not knowing
how blind that was.

Lovers don't finally meet somewhere,
they're in each other all along.
Love is from the infinite, and will remain until eternity.
The seeker of love escapes the chains of birth and death.
Tomorrow, when resurrection comes,
The heart that is not in love will fail the test.

When I am with you, we stay up all night,
When you're not here, I can't get to sleep.
Praise God for these two insomnias!
And the difference between them.

Suddenly the drunken sweetheart appeared out of my door.
She drank a cup of ruby wine and sat by my side.
Seeing and holding the lockets of her hair
My face became all eyes, and my eyes all hands.

I have phrases and whole pages memorized,
but nothing can be told of love.
You must wait until you and I
are living together.
In the conversation we'll have
then...be patient...then.

A Smile and A Gentleness:

There is a smile and a gentleness
inside. When I learned the name
and address of that, I went to where
you sell perfume. I begged you not
to trouble me so with longing. Come
out and play! Flirt more naturally.
Teach me how to kiss. On the ground
a spread blanket, flame that's caught
and burning well, cumin seeds browning,
I am inside all of this with my soul.

When the sweet glance of my true love caught my eyes,
Like alchemy, it transformed my copper-like soul.
I searched for Him with a thousand hands,
He stretched out His arms and clutched my feet.

With the Beloved's water of life, no illness remains
In the Beloved's rose garden of union, no thorn remains.
They say there is a window from one heart to another
How can there be a window where no wall remains?

Let the lover be disgraceful, crazy,
absentminded. Someone sober
will worry about things going badly.
Let the lover be.

When your chest is free of your limiting ego,
Then you will see the ageless Beloved.
You can not see yourself without a mirror;
Look at the Beloved, He is the brightest mirror.

The Freshness:

When it's cold and raining,
you are more beautiful.
And the snow brings me
even closer to your lips.
The inner secret, that which was never born,
you are that freshness, and I am with you now.
I can't explain the goings,
or the comings. You enter suddenly,
and I am nowhere again.
Inside the majesty.

Some Kiss We Want:

There is some kiss we want with
our whole lives, the touch of
spirit on the body. Seawater
begs the pearl to break its shell.
And the lily, how passionately
it needs some wild darling! At
night, I open the window and ask
the moon to come and press its
face against mine. Breathe into
me. Close the language- door and
open the love window. The moon
won't use the door, only the window.

150

Another Muslim mystic is the Persian poet Khwāja Shams-ud-Dīn Muhammad Hāfez-e Shīrāzī, known by his pen name Hāfez or Hāfiz. He lived between cir. 1325 and 1390. CE

His collected works are regarded as a pinnacle of Persian literature and are to be found in the homes of most people in Iran, who learn his poems by heart and use them as proverbs and sayings.

Themes of his poems are the beloved, faith, and his sharp insights exposing hypocrisy, especially in the religious community. His influence in the lives of Persian speakers can be found in "Hafez readings". His works are frequently used in Persian traditional music, visual art, and Persian calligraphy.

Below are a few of the poems of Hafiz.
Translated by Gertrude Lowthian Bell [1897]

TEACHINGS OF HAFIZ

I

ARISE, oh Cup-bearer, rise! and bring
To lips that are thirsting the bowl they praise,
For it seemed that love was an easy thing,
But my feet have fallen on difficult ways.
I have prayed the wind o'er my heart to fling
The fragrance of musk in her hair that sleeps
In the night of her hair-yet no fragrance stays
The tears of my heart's blood my sad heart weeps.

Hear the Tavern-keeper who counsels you:
"With wine, with red wine your prayer carpet dye!"
There was never a traveller like him but knew
The ways of the road and the hostelry.
Where shall I rest, when the still night through,
Beyond thy gateway, oh Heart of my heart,
The bells of the camels lament and cry:
"Bind up thy burden again and depart!"

The waves run high, night is clouded with fears,
And eddying whirlpools clash and roar;
How shall my drowning voice strike their ears
Whose light-freighted vessels have reached the shore?
I sought mine own; the unsparing years
Have brought me mine own, a dishonoured name.
What cloak shall cover my misery o'er
When each jesting mouth has rehearsed my shame!
Oh Hafiz, seeking an end to strife,
Hold fast in thy mind what the wise have writ:
"If at last thou attain the desire of thy life,
Cast the world aside, yea, abandon it!"

II

THE bird of gardens sang unto the rose,
New blown in the clear dawn: "Bow down thy head!
As fair as thou within this garden close,
Many have bloomed and died." She laughed and said
"That I am born to fade grieves not my heart
But never was it a true lover's part
To vex with bitter words his love's repose."

The tavern step shall be thy hostelry,
For Love's diviner breath comes but to those
That suppliant on the dusty threshold lie.
And thou, if thou would'st drink the wine that flows
From Life's bejewelled goblet, ruby red,

Upon thine eyelashes thine eyes shall thread
A thousand tears for this temerity.

Last night when Irem's magic garden slept,
Stirring the hyacinth's purple tresses curled,
The wind of morning through the alleys stept.
"Where is thy cup, the mirror of the world?
Ah, where is Love, thou Throne of Djem?" I cried.
The breezes knew not; but "Alas," they sighed,
"That happiness should sleep so long!" and wept.

Not on the lips of men Love's secret lies,
Remote and unrevealed his dwelling-place.
Oh Saki, come! the idle laughter dies
When thou the feast with heavenly wine dost grace.
Patience and wisdom, Hafiz, in a sea
Of thine own tears are drowned; thy misery
They could not still nor hide from curious eyes.

III

WIND from the east, oh Lapwing of the day,
I send thee to my Lady, though the way
Is far to Saba, where I bid thee fly;
Lest in the dust thy tameless wings should lie,
Broken with grief, I send thee to thy nest,
Fidelity.

Or far or near there is no halting-place
Upon Love's road-absent, I see thy face,
And in thine car my wind-blown greetings sound,
North winds and east waft them where they are bound,
Each morn and eve convoys of greeting fair
I send to thee.

Unto mine eyes a stranger, thou that art

A comrade ever-present to my heart,
What whispered prayers and what full meed of praise
I send to thee.

Lest Sorrow's army waste thy heart's domain,
I send my life to bring thee peace again,
Dear life thy ransom! From thy singers learn
How one that longs for thee may weep and bum
Sonnets and broken words, sweet notes and songs
I send to thee.

Give me the cup! a voice rings in mine cars
Crying: "Bear patiently the bitter years!
For all thine ills, I send thee heavenly grace.
God the Creator mirrored in thy face
Thine eyes shall see, God's image in the glass
I send to thee.

Hafiz, thy praise alone my comrades sing;
Hasten to us, thou that art sorrowing!
A robe of honour and a harnessed steed
I send to thee."

IV

SLEEP on thine eyes, bright as narcissus flowers,
Falls not in vain
And not in vain thy hair's soft radiance showers
Ah, not in vain!

Before the milk upon thy lips was dry,
I said: "Lips where the salt of wit doth lie,
Sweets shall be mingled with thy mockery,
And not in vain!"

Thy mouth the fountain where Life's waters flow,
A dimpled well of tears is set below,

And death lies near to life thy lovers know,
But know in vain!

God send to thee great length of happy days
Lo, not for his own life thy servant prays;
Love's dart in thy bent brows the Archer lays,
Nor shoots in vain.

Art thou with grief afflicted, with the smart
Of absence, and is bitter toil thy part?
Thy lamentations and thy tears, oh Heart,
Are not in vain

Last night the wind from out her village blew,
And wandered all the garden alleys through,
Oh rose, tearing thy bosom's robe in two;
'Twas not in vain!

And Hafiz, though thy heart within thee dies,
Hiding love's agony from curious eyes,
Ah, not in vain thy tears, not vain thy sighs,
Not all in vain

V

OH Turkish maid of Shiraz! in thy hand
If thou'lt take my heart, for the mole on thy cheek
I would barter Bokhara and Samarkand.
Bring, Cup-bearer, all that is left of thy wine!
In the Garden of Paradise vainly thou'lt seek
The lip of the fountain of Ruknabad,
And the bowers of Mosalla where roses twine.

They have filled the city with blood and broil,
Those soft-voiced Lulis for whom we sigh;
As Turkish robbers fall on the spoil,

They have robbed and plundered the peace of my heart.
Dowered is my mistress, a beggar am I;
What shall I bring her? a beautiful face
Needs nor jewel nor mole nor the tiring-maid's art.

Brave tales of singers and wine relate,
The key to the Hidden 'twere vain to seek;
No wisdom of ours has unlocked that gate,
And locked to our wisdom it still shall be.
But of Joseph's beauty the lute shall speak;
And the minstrel knows that Zuleika came forth,
Love parting the curtains of modesty.

When thou spokest ill of thy servant 'twas well--
God pardon thee! for thy words were sweet;
Not unwelcomed the bitterest answer fell
From lips where the ruby and sugar lay.
But, fair Love, let good counsel direct thy feet;
Far dearer to youth than dear life itself
Are the warnings of one grown wise--and grey!

The song is sung and the pearl is strung
Come hither, oh Hafiz, and sing again!
And the listening Heavens above thee hung
Shall loose o'er thy verse the Pleiades' chain.

VI

A FLOWER-TINTED cheek, the flowery close
Of the fair earth, these are enough for me
Enough that in the meadow wanes and grows
The shadow of a graceful cypress-tree.
I am no lover of hypocrisy;
Of all the treasures that the earth can boast,
A brimming cup of wine I prize the most--
This is enough for me!

To them that here renowned for virtue live,
A heavenly palace is the meet reward;
To me, the drunkard and the beggar, give
The temple of the grape with red wine stored!
Beside a river seat thee on the sward;
It floweth past-so flows thy life away,
So sweetly, swiftly, fleets our little day--
Swift, but enough for me!

Look upon all the gold in the world's mart,
On all the tears the world hath shed in vain
Shall they not satisfy thy craving heart?
I have enough of loss, enough of gain;
I have my Love, what more can I obtain?
Mine is the joy of her companionship
Whose healing lip is laid upon my lip--
This is enough for me!

I pray thee send not forth my naked soul
From its poor house to seek for Paradise
Though heaven and earth before me God unroll,
Back to thy village still my spirit flies.
And, Hafiz, at the door of Kismet lies
No just complaint-a mind like water clear,
A song that swells and dies upon the ear,
These are enough for thee!

VII

FROM the garden of Heaven a western breeze
Blows through the leaves of my garden of earth;
With a love like a huri I'll take mine ease,
And wine! bring me wine, the giver of mirth!
Today the beggar may boast him a king,
His banqueting-hall is the ripening field,
And his tent the shadow that soft clouds fling.

A tale of April the meadows unfold--
Ah, foolish for future credit to slave,
And to leave the cash of the present untold!
Build a fort with wine where thy heart may brave
The assault of the world; when thy fortress falls,
The relentless victor shall knead from thy dust
The bricks that repair its crumbling walls.

Trust not the word of that foe in the fight!
Shall the lamp of the synagogue lend its flame
To set thy monastic torches alight?
Drunken am I, yet place not my name
In the Book of Doom, nor pass judgment on it;
Who knows what the secret finger of Fate
Upon his own white forehead has writ!

And when the spirit of Hafiz has fled,
Follow his bier with a tribute of sighs;
Though the ocean of sin has closed o'er his head,
He may find a place in God's Paradise.

VIII

The rose has flushed red, the bud has burst,
And drunk with joy is the nightingale
Hail, Sufis! lovers of wine, all hail!
For wine is proclaimed to a world athirst.
Like a rock your repentance seemed to you;
Behold the marvel! of what avail
Was your rock, for a goblet has cleft it in two!

Bring wine for the king and the slave at the gate
Alike for all is the banquet spread,
And drunk and sober are warmed and fed.
When the feast is done and the night grows late,
And the second door of the tavern gapes wide,

The low and. the mighty must bow the head
'Neath the archway of Life, to meet what . . . outside?

Except thy road through affliction pass,
None may reach the halting-station of mirth
God's treaty: Am I not Lord of the earth?
Man sealed with a sigh: Ah yes, alas!
Nor with Is nor Is Not let thy mind contend
Rest assured all perfection of mortal birth
In the great Is Not at the last shall end.

For Assaf's pomp, and the steeds of the wind,
And the speech of birds, down the wind have fled,
And he that was lord of them all is dead;
Of his mastery nothing remains behind.
Shoot not thy feathered arrow astray!
A bow-shot's length through the air it has sped,
And then . . . dropped down in the dusty way.

But to thee, oh Hafiz, to thee, oh Tongue
That speaks through the mouth of the slender reed,
What thanks to thee when thy verses speed
From lip to lip, and the song thou hast sung?

IX

OH Cup-bearer, set my glass afire
With the light of wine! oh minstrel, sing:
The world fulfilleth my heart's desire!
Reflected within the goblet's ring
I see the glow of my Love's red cheek,
And scant of wit, ye who fail to seek
The pleasures that wine alone can bring!

Let not the blandishments be checked
That slender beauties lavish on me,

159

Until in the grace of the cypress decked,
My Love shall come like a ruddy pine-tree
He cannot perish whose heart doth hold
The life love breathes-though my days are told,
In the Book of the World lives my constancy.

But when the Day of Reckoning is here,
I fancy little will be the gain
That accrues to the Sheikh for his lawful cheer,
Or to me for the draught forbidden I drain.
The drunken eyes of my comrades shine,
And I too, stretching my hand to the wine,
On the neck of drunkenness loosen the rein.

Oh wind, if thou passest the garden close
Of my heart's dear master, carry for me
The message I send to him, wind that blows!
"Why hast thou thrust from thy memory
My hapless name?" breathe low in his ear;
"Knowest thou not that the day is near
When nor thou nor any shall think on me?"

If with tears, oh Hafiz, thine eyes are wet,
Scatter them round thee like grain, and snare
The Bird of joy when it comes to thy net.
As the tulip shrinks from the cold night air,
So shrank my heart and quailed in the shade
Oh Song-bird Fortune, the toils are laid,
When shall thy bright wings lie pinioned there?

The heavens' green sea and the bark therein,
The slender bark of the crescent moon,
Are lost in thy bounty's radiant noon,
Vizir and pilgrim, Kawameddin!

X

SINGER, sweet Singer, fresh notes strew,
Fresh and afresh and new and new!
Heart-gladdening wine thy lips imbrue,
Fresh and afresh and new and new!

Saki, thy radiant feet I hail;
Flush with red wine the goblets pale,
Flush our pale cheeks to drunken hue,
Fresh and afresh and new and new!

Then with thy love to toy with thee,
Rest thee, ah, rest! where none can see
Seek thy delight, for kisses sue,
Fresh and afresh and new and new!

Here round thy life the vine is twined;
Drink I for elsewhere what wine wilt find?
Drink to her name, to hours that flew,
Hours ever fresh and new and new!

She that has stolen my heart from me,
How does she wield her empery?
Paints and adorns and scents her too,
Fresh and afresh and new and new!

Wind of the dawn that passest by,
Swift to the street of my fairy hie,
Whisper the tale of Hafiz true,
Fresh and afresh and new and new!

XI

MIRTH, Spring, to linger in a garden fair,

What more has earth to give? All ye that wait,
Where is the Cup-bearer, the flagon where?
When pleasant hours slip from the hand of Fate,
Reckon each hour as a certain gain;
Who seeks to know the end of mortal care
Shall question his experience in vain.

Thy fettered life hangs on a single thread--
Some comfort for thy present ills devise,
But those that time may bring thou shalt not dread.
Waters of Life and Irem's Paradise--
What meaning do our dreams and pomp convey,
Save that beside a mighty stream, wide-fed,
We sit and sing of wine and go our way!

The modest and the merry shall be seen
To boast their kinship with a single voice;
There are no differences to choose between,
Thou art but flattering thy soul with choice!
Who knows the Curtain's secret? . . . Heaven is mute
And yet with Him who holds the Curtain, even
With Him, oh Braggart, thou would'st raise dispute!

Although His thrall shall miss the road and err,
'Tis but to teach him wisdom through distress,
Else Pardon and Compassionate Mercy were
But empty syllables and meaningless.
The Zealot thirsts for draughts of Kausar's wine,
And Hafiz doth an earthly cup prefer--
But what, between the two, is God's design?

XII

WHERE is my ruined life, and where the fame
Of noble deeds?
Look on my long-drawn road, and whence it came,
And where it leads!

162

Can drunkenness be linked to piety
And good repute?
Where is the preacher's holy monody,
Where is the lute?

From monkish cell and lying garb released,
Oh heart of mine,
Where is the Tavern fane, the Tavern priest,
Where is the wine?

Past days of meeting, let the memory
Of you be sweet!
Where are those glances fled, and where for me
Reproaches meet?

His friend's bright face warms not the enemy
When love is done--
Where is the extinguished lamp that made night day,
Where is the sun?

Balm to mine eyes the dust, my head I bow
Upon thy stair.
Where shall I go, where from thy presence? thou
Art everywhere.

Look not upon the dimple of her chin,
Danger lurks there!
Where wilt thou hide, oh trembling heart, fleeing in
Such mad haste--where?

To steadfastness and patience, friend, ask not
If Hafiz keep--
Patience and steadfastness I have forgot,
And where is sleep?

XIII

LADY that hast my heart within thy hand,
Thou heed'st me not; and if thou turn thine ear
Unto the wise, thou shalt not understand--
Behold the fault is thine, our words were clear.
For all the tumult in my drunken brain
Praise God! who trieth not His slave in vain;
Nor this world nor the next shall make me fear!

My weary heart eternal silence keeps--
I know not who has slipped into my heart;
Though I am silent, one within me weeps.
My soul shall rend the painted veil apart.
Where art thou, Minstrel! touch thy saddest strings
Till clothed in music such as sorrow sings,
My mournful story from thy zither sweeps.

Lo, not at any time I lent mine ear
To hearken to the glories of the earth;
Only thy beauty to mine eyes was dear.
Sleep has forsaken me, and from the birth
Of night till day I weave bright dreams of thee;
Drunk with a hundred nights of revelry,
Where is the tavern that sets forth such cheer!

My heart, sad hermit, stains the cloister floor
With drops of blood, the sweat of anguish dire;
Ah, wash me clean, and o'er my body pour
Love's generous wine! the worshippers of fire
Have bowed them down and magnified my name,
For in my heart there burns a living flame,
Transpiercing Death's impenetrable door.

What instrument through last night's silence rang?
My life into his lay the minstrel wove,

164

And filled my brain with the sweet song he sang.
It was the proclamation of thy love
That shook the strings of Life's most secret lyre,
And still my breast heaves with last night's desire,
For countless echoes from that music sprang.

And ever, since the time that Hafiz heard
His Lady's voice, as from a rocky hill
Reverberates the softly spoken word,
So echoes of desire his bosom fill.

XIV

THE nightingale with drops of his heart's blood
Had nourished the red rose, then came a wind,
And catching at the boughs in envious mood,
A hundred thorns about his heart entwined.
Like to the parrot crunching sugar, good
Seemed the world to me who could not stay
The wind of Death that swept my hopes away.

Light of mine eyes and harvest of my heart,
And mine at least in changeless memory!
Ah, when he found it easy to depart,
He left the harder pilgrimage to me!
Oh Camel-driver, though the cordage start,
For God's sake help me lift my fallen load,
And Pity be my comrade of the road!

My face is seamed with dust, mine eyes are wet.
Of dust and tears the turquoise firmament
Kneadeth the bricks for joy's abode; and yet . . .
Alas, and weeping yet I make lament!
Because the moon her jealous glances set
Upon the bow-bent eyebrows of my moon,
He sought a lodging in the grave-too soon!

I had not castled, and the time is gone.
What shall I play? Upon the chequered floor
Of Night and Day, Death won the game-forlorn
And careless now, Hafiz can lose no more.

XV

RETURN! that to a heart wounded full sore
Valiance and strength may enter in; return!
And Life shall pause at the deserted door,
The cold dead body breathe again and burn.
Oh come! and touch mine eyes, of thy sweet grace,
For I am blind to all but to thy face.
Open the gates and bid me see once more!

Like to a cruel Ethiopian band,
Sorrow despoiled the kingdom of my heart
Return! glad Lord of Rome, and free the land;
Before thine arms the foe shall break and part.
See now, I hold a mirror to mine eyes,
And nought but thy reflection therein lies;
The glass speaks truth to them that understand.

Night is with child, hast thou not heard men say?
"Night is with child! what will she bring to birth?"
I sit and ask the stars when thou'rt away.
Oh come! and when the nightingale of mirth
Pipes in the Spring-awakened garden ground,
In Hafiz' heart shall ring a sweeter sound,
Diviner nightingales attune their lay.

XVI

WHAT is wrought in the forge of the living and life--
All things are nought! Ho! fill me the bowl,
For nought is the gear of the world and the strife!

166

One passion has quickened the heart and the soul,
The Beloved's presence alone they have sought--
Love at least exists; yet if Love were not,
Heart and soul would sink to the common lot--
All things are nought!

Like an empty cup is the fate of each,
That each must fill from Life's mighty flood;
Nought thy toil, though to Paradise gate thou reach,
If Another has filled up thy cup with blood;
Neither shade from the sweet-fruited trees could be bought
By thy praying-oh Cypress of Truth, dost not see
That Sidreh and Tuba were nought, and to thee
All then were nought!

The span of thy life is as five little days,
Brief hours and swift in this halting-place;
Rest softly, ah rest! while the Shadow delays,
For Time's self is nought and the dial's face.
On the lip of Oblivion we linger, and short
Is the way from the Lip to the Mouth where we pass
While the moment is thine, fill, oh Saki, the glass
Ere all is nought!

Consider the rose that breaks into flower,
Neither repines though she fade and die--
The powers of the world endure for an hour,
But nought shall remain of their majesty.
Be not too sure of your crown, you who thought
That virtue was easy and recompense yours;
From the monastery to the wine-tavern doors
The way is nought

What though I, too, have tasted the salt of my tears,
Though I, too, have burnt in the fires of grief,
Shall I cry aloud to unheeding ears?

Mourn and be silent! nought brings relief.
Thou, Hafiz, art praised for the songs thou hast wrought,
But bearing a stained or an honoured name,
The lovers of wine shall make light of thy fame--
All things are nought!

XVII

LAY not reproach at the drunkard's door
Oh Fanatic, thou that art pure of soul;
Not thine on the page of life to enrol
The faults of others! Or less or more
I have swerved from my path--keep thou to thine own
For every man when he reaches the goal
Shall reap the harvest his hands have sown.

Leave me the hope of a former grace--
Till the curtain is lifted none can tell
Whether in Heaven or deepest Hell,
Fair or vile, shall appear his face.
Alike the drunk and the strict of fare
For his mistress yearns--in the mosque Love doth dwell
And the church, for his lodging is everywhere.

If without the house of devotion I stand,
I am not the first to throw wide the door
My father opened it long before,
The eternal Paradise slipped from his hand.
All you that misconstrue my words' intent,
I lie on the bricks of the tavern floor,
And a brick shall serve me for argument.

Heaven's garden future treasures may yield--
Ah, make the most of earth's treasury!
The flickering shade of the willow-tree,
And the grass-grown lip of the fruitful field.
Trust not in deeds--the Eternal Day

Shall reveal the Creator's sentence on thee;
But till then, what His finger has writ, who can say.

Bring the cup in thine hand to the Judgment-seat;
Thou shalt rise, oh Hafiz, to Heaven's gate
From the tavern where thou hast tarried late.
And if thou hast worshipped wine, thou shalt meet
The reward that the Faithful attain;
If such thy life, then fear not thy fate,
Thou shalt not have lived and worshipped in vain.

XVIII

Slaves of thy shining eyes are even those
That diadems of might and empire bear;
Drunk with the wine that from thy red lip flows,
Are they that even the grape's delight forswear.
Drift, like the wind across a violet bed,
Before thy many lovers, weeping low,
And clad like violets in blue robes of woe,
Who feel thy wind-blown hair and bow the head.

Thy messenger the breath of dawn, and mine
A stream of tears, since lover and beloved
Keep not their secret; through my verses shine,
Though other lays my flower's grace have proved
And countless nightingales have sung thy praise.
When veiled beneath thy curls thou passest, see,
To right and leftward those that welcome thee
Have bartered peace and rest on thee to gaze!

But thou that knowest God by heart, away!
Wine-drunk, love-drunk, we inherit Paradise,
His mercy is for sinners; hence and pray
Where wine thy cheek red as red erghwan dyes,
And leave the cell to faces sinister.

Oh Khizr, whose happy feet bathed in life's fount,
Help one who toils afoot-the horsemen mount
And hasten on their way; I scarce can stir.

Ah, loose me not! ah, set not Hafiz free
From out the bondage of thy gleaming hair!
Safe only those, safe, and at liberty,
That fast enchained in thy linked ringlets are.
But from the image of his dusty cheek
Learn this from Hafiz: proudest heads shall bend,
And dwellers on the threshold of a friend
Be crownèd with the dust that crowns the meek.

XIX

WHAT drunkenness is this that brings me hope--
Who was the Cup-bearer, and whence the wine?
That minstrel singing with full voice divine,
What lay was his? for 'mid the woven rope
Of song, he brought word from my Friend to me
Set to his melody.

The wind itself bore joy to Solomon;
The Lapwing flew from Sheba's garden close,
Bringing good tidings of its queen and rose.
Take thou the cup and go where meadows span
The plain, whither the bird with tuneful throat
Has brought Spring's sweeter note.

Welcome, oh rose, and full-blown eglantine!
The violets their scented gladness fling,
Jasmine breathes purity-art sorrowing
Like an unopened bud, oh heart of mine?
The wind of dawn that sets closed blossoms free
Brings its warm airs to thee.

Saki, thy kiss shall still my bitter cry!

Lift up your grief-bowed heads, all ye that weep,
The Healer brings joy's wine-cup--oh, drink deep!
Disciple of the Tavern-priest am I;
The pious Sheikh may promise future bliss,
He brings me where joy is.

The greedy glances of a Tartar horde
To me seemed kind--my foeman spared me not
Though one poor robe was all that I had got.
But Heaven served Hafiz, as a slave his lord,
And when he fled through regions desolate,
Heaven brought him to thy gate.

XX

From out the street of So-and-So,
Oh wind, bring perfumes sweet to me
For I am sick and pale with woe;
Oh bring me rest from misery!
The dust that lies before her door,
Love's long desired elixir, pour
Upon this wasted heart of mine--
Bring me a promise and a sign!

Between the ambush of mine eyes
And my heart's fort there is enmity--
Her eye-brow's bow, the dart that flies,
Beneath her lashes, bring to me!
Sorrow and absence, glances cold,
Before my time have made me old;
A wine-cup from the hand of Youth
Bring me for pity and for Ruth!

Then shall all unbelievers taste
A draught or two of that same wine;
But if they like it not, oh haste!

And let joy's flowing cup be mine.
Cup-bearer, seize to-day, nor wait
Until to-morrow!--or from Fate
Some passport to felicity,
Some written surety bring to me!

My heart threw back the veil of woe,
Consoled by Hafiz melody:
From out the street of So-and-So,
Oh wind, bring perfumes sweet to me!

XXI

Not all the sum of earthly happiness
Is worth the bowed head of a moment's pain,
And if I sell for wine my dervish dress,
Worth more than what I sell is what I gain!
Land where my Lady dwells, thou holdest me
Enchained; else Fars were but a barren soil,
Not worth the journey over land and sea,
Not worth the toil!

Down in the quarter where they sell red wine,
My holy carpet scarce would fetch a cup
How brave a pledge of piety is mine,
Which is not worth a goblet foaming up!
Mine enemy heaped scorn on me and said
"Forth from the tavern gate!" Why am I thrust
From off the threshold? is my fallen head
Not worth the dust?

Wash white that travel-stained sad robe of thine!
Where word and deed alike one colour bear,
The grape's fair purple garment shall outshine
Thy many-coloured rags and tattered gear.
Full easy seemed the sorrow of the sea
Lightened by hope of gain--hope flew too fast

A hundred pearls were poor indemnity,
Not worth the blast.

The Sultan's crown, with priceless jewels set,
Encircles fear of death and constant dread
It is a head-dress much desired--and yet
Art sure 'tis worth the danger to the head?
It was best for thee to hide thy face from those
That long for thee; the Conqueror's reward
Is never worth the army's long-drawn woes,
Worth fire and sword.

Ah, seek the treasure of a mind at rest
And store it in the treasury of Ease;
Not worth a loyal heart, a tranquil breast,
Were all the riches of thy lands and seas!
Ah, scorn, like Hafiz, the delights of earth,
Ask not one grain of favour from the base,
Two hundred sacks of jewels were not worth
Thy soul's disgrace

XXII

The rose is not fair without the beloved's face,
Nor merry the Spring without the sweet laughter of wine;
The path through the fields, and winds from a flower strewn
place,
Without her bright check, which glows like a tulip fine,
Nor winds softly blowing, fields deep in corn, are fair.

And lips like to sugar, grace like a flower that sways,
Are nought without kisses many and dalliance sweet;
If thousands of voices sang not the rose's praise,
The joy of the cypress her opening bud to greet,
Nor dancing of boughs nor blossoming rose were fair.

Though limned by most skilful fingers, no pictures please
Unless the beloved's image is drawn therein;
The garden and flowers, and hair flowing loose on the breeze,
Unless to my Lady's side I may strive and win,
Nor garden, nor flowers, nor loose flying curls are fair.

Hast seen at a marriage-feast, when the mirth runs high,
The revellers scatter gold with a careless hand?
The gold of thy heart, oh Hafiz, despised doth lie,
Not worthy thy love to be cast by a drunken band
At the feet of her who is fairer than all that's fair.

XXIII

My lady, that did change this house of mine
Into a heaven when that she dwelt therein,
From head to foot an angel's grace divine
Enwrapped her; pure she was, spotless of sin;
Fair as the moon her countenance, and wise;
Lords of the kind and tender glance, her eyes
With an abounding loveliness did shine.

Then said my heart: Here will I take my rest!
This city breathes her love in every part.
But to a distant bourne was she addressed,
Alas! he knew it not, alas, poor heart!
The influence of some cold malignant star
Has loosed my hand that held her, lone and far
She journeyeth that lay upon my breast.

Not only did she lift my bosom's veil,
Reveal its inmost secret, but her grace
Drew back the curtain from Heaven's mansions pale,
And gave her there an eternal dwelling-place.
The flower-strewn river lip and meadows fair,
The rose herself but fleeting treasures were,
Regret and Winter follow in their trail.

Dear were the days which perished with my friend--
Ah, what is left of life, now she is dead,
All wisdomless and profitless I spend!
The nightingale his own life's blood doth shed,
When, to the kisses of the wind, the morn
Unveils the rose's splendour-with his torn
And jealous breast he dyes her petals red.

Yet pardon her, oh Heart, for poor wert thou,
A humble dervish on the dusty way;
Crowned with the crown of empire was her brow,
And in the realms of beauty she bore sway.
But all the joy that Hafiz' hand might hold,
Lay in the beads that morn and eve he told,
Worn with God's praise; and see! he holds it now.

XXIV

Not one is filled with madness like to mine
In all the taverns! my soiled robe lies here,
There my neglected book, both pledged for wine.
With dust my heart is thick, that should be clear,
A glass to mirror forth the Great King's face;
One ray of light from out Thy dwelling-place
To pierce my night, oh God! and draw me near.

From out mine eyes unto my garment's hem
A river flows; perchance my cypress-tree
Beside that stream may rear her lofty stem,
Watering her roots with tears. Ah, bring to me
The wine vessel! since my Love's cheek is hid,
A flood of grief comes from my heart unbid,
And turns mine eyes into a bitter sea!

Nay, by the hand that sells me wine, I vow

No more the brimming cup shall touch my lips,
Until my mistress with her radiant brow
Adorns my feast-until Love's secret slips
From her, as from the candle's tongue of flame,
Though I, the singèd moth, for very shame,
Dare not extol Love's light without eclipse.

Red wine I worship, and I worship her--
Speak not to me of anything beside,
For nought but these on earth or heaven I care.
What though the proud narcissus flowers defied
Thy shining eyes to prove themselves more bright,
Yet heed them not! those that are clear of sight
Follow not them to whom all light's denied.

Before the tavern door a Christian sang
To sound of pipe and drum, what time the earth
Awaited the white dawn, and gaily rang
Upon mine ear those harbingers of mirth:
"If the True Faith be such as thou dost say,
Alas! my Hafiz, that this sweet To-day
Should bring unknown To-morrow to the birth!"

XXV

The days of absence and the bitter nights
Of separation, all are at an end!
Where is the influence of the star that blights
My hope? The omen answers: At an end!
Autumn's abundance, creeping Autumn's mirth,
Are ended and forgot when o'er the earth
The wind of Spring with soft warm feet doth wend.

The Day of Hope, hid beneath Sorrow's veil,
Has shown its face--ah, cry that all may hear:
Come forth! the powers of night no more prevail!
Praise be to God, now that the rose is near

With long-desired and flaming coronet,
The cruel stinging thorns all men forget,
The wind of Winter ends its proud career.

The long confusion of the nights that were,
Anguish that dwelt within my heart, is o'er;
'Neath the protection of my lady's hair
Grief nor disquiet come to me no more.
What though her curls wrought all my misery,
My lady's gracious face can comfort me,
And at the end give what I sorrow for.

Light-hearted to the tavern let me go,
Where laughs the pipe, the merry cymbals kiss;
Under the history of all my woe,
My mistress sets her hand and writes: Finis.
Oh, linger not, nor trust the inconstant days
That promised: Where thou art thy lady stays--
The tale of separation ends with this!

Joy's certain path, oh Saki, thou hast shown--
Long may thy cup be full, thy days be fair!
Trouble and sickness from my breast have flown,
Order and health thy wisdom marshals there.
Not one that numbered Hafiz' name among
The great-unnumbered were his tears, unsung;
Praise him that sets an end to endless care!

XXVI

THE secret draught of wine and love repressed
Are joys foundationless--then come whatever
May come, slave to the grape I stand confessed!
Unloose, oh friend, the knot of thy heart's care,
Despite the warning that the Heavens reveal!
For all his thought, never astronomer

That loosed the knot of Fate those Heavens conceal!

Not all the changes that thy days unfold
Shall rouse thy wonder; Time's revolving sphere
Over a thousand lives like thine has rolled.
That cup within thy fingers, dost not hear
The voices of dead kings speak through the clay
Kobad, Bahman, Djemshid, their dust is here,
"Gently upon me set thy lips!" they say.

What man can tell where Kaus and Kai have gone?
Who knows where even now the restless wind
Scatters the dust of Djem's imperial throne?
And where the tulip, following close behind
The feet of Spring, her scarlet chalice rears,
There Ferhad for the love of Shirin pined,
Dyeing the desert red with his heart's tears.

Bring, bring the cup! drink we while yet we may
To our soul's ruin the forbidden draught
Perhaps a treasure-trove is hid away
Among those ruins where the wine has laughed!--
Perhaps the tulip knows the fickleness
Of Fortune's smile, for on her stalk's green shaft
She bears a wine-cup through the wilderness.

The murmuring stream of Ruknabad, the breeze
That blows from out Mosalla's fair pleasaunce,
Summon me back when I would seek heart's ease,
Travelling afar; what though Love's countenance
Be turned full harsh and sorrowful on me,
I care not so that Time's unfriendly glance
Still from my Lady's beauty turned be.

Like Hafiz, drain the goblet cheerfully
While minstrels touch the lute and sweetly sing,
For all that makes thy heart rejoice in thee

Hangs of Life's single, slender, silken string.

XXVII

My friend has fled! alas, my friend has fled,
And left me nought but tears and pain behind!
Like smoke above a flame caught by the wind,
So rose she from my breast and forth she sped.
Drunk with desire, I seized Love's cup divine,
But she that held it poured the bitter wine
Of Separation into it and fled.

The hunter she, and I the helpless prey;
Wounded and sick, round me her toils she drew,
My heart into a sea of sorrow threw,
Bound up her camel loads and fled away.
Fain had I laid an ambush for her soul,
She saw and vanished, and the timid foal,
Good Fortune, slipped the rein and would not stay.

My heart was all too narrow for my woe,
And tears of blood my weeping eyes have shed,
A crimson stream across the desert sped,
Rising from out my sad heart's overflow.
She knew not what Love's meanest slave can tell:
"'Tis sweet to serve!" but threw me a Farewell,
Kissing my threshold, turned, and cried "I go!"

In the clear dawn, before the east was red,
Before the rose had torn her veil in two,
A nightingale through Hafiz' garden flew,
Stayed but to fill its song with tears, and fled.

XXVIII

Hast thou forgotten when thy stolen glance

Was turned to me, when on my happy face
Clearly thy love was writ, which doth enhance
All happiness? or when my sore disgrace
(Hast thou forgot?) drew from thine eyes reproof,
And made thee hold thy sweet red lips aloof,
Dowered, like Jesus's breath, with healing grace?

Hast thou forgotten how the glorious
Swift nights flew past, the cup of dawn brimmed high?
My love and I alone, God favouring us!
Andwhen she like a waning moon did lie,
And Steep had drawn his coif about her brow,
Hast thou forgot? Heaven's crescent moon would bow
The head, and in her service pace the sky!

Hast thou forgotten, when a sojourner
Within the tavern gates and drunk with wine,
I found Love's passionate wisdom hidden there,
Which in the mosque none even now divine?
The goblet's carbuncle (hast thou forgot?)
Laughed out aloud, and speech flew hot
And fast between thy ruby lips and mine!

Hast thou forgotten when thy cheek's dear torch
Lighted the beacon of desire in me,
And when my heart, like foolish moths that scorch
Their wings and yet return, turned all to thee?
Within the banquet-hall of Good Repute
(Hast thou forgot?) the wine's self-pressed my suit,
And filled the morn with drunken jollity!

Hast thou forgotten when thou laid'st aright
The uncut gems of Hafiz' inmost thought,
And side by side thy sweet care strung the bright
Array of verse on verse-hast thou forgot?

XXIX

FROM Canaan Joseph shall return, whose face
A little time was hidden: weep no more--
Oh, weep no more! in sorrow's dwelling-place
The roses yet shall spring from the bare floor!
And heart bowed down beneath a secret pain--
Oh stricken heart! joy shall return again,
Peace to the love-tossed brain--oh, weep no more!

Oh, weep no more! for once again Life's Spring
Shall throne her in the meadows green, and o'er
Her head the minstrel of the night shall fling
A canopy of rose leaves, score on score.
The secret of the world thou shalt not learn,
And yet behind the veil Love's fire may burn--
Weepest thou? let hope return and weep no more!

To-day may pass, to-morrow pass, before
The turning wheel give me my heart's desire;
Heaven's self shall change, and turn not evermore
The universal wheel of Fate in ire.
Oh Pilgrim nearing Mecca's holy fane,
The thorny mageilan wounds thee in vain,
The desert blooms again--oh, weep no more!

What though the river of mortality
Round the unstable house of Life doth roar,
Weep not, oh heart, Noah shall pilot thee,
And guide thine ark to the desirèd shore!
The goal lies far, and perilous is thy road,
Yet every path leads to that same abode
Where thou shalt drop thy load--oh, weep no more!

Mine enemies have persecuted me,

My Love has turned and fled from out my door--
God counts our tears and knows our misery;
Ah, weep not! He has heard thy weeping sore.
And chained in poverty and plunged in night,
Oh Hafiz, take thy Koran and recite
Litanies infinite, and weep no more!

XXX

ALL hail, Shiraz, hail! oh site without peer!
May God be the Watchman before thy gate,
That the feet of Misfortune enter not here!
Lest my Ruknabad be left desolate,
A hundred times, "God forbid!" I pray;
Its limpid stream where the shadows wait
Like the fount of Khizr giveth life for aye.

'Twixt Jafrabad and Mosalla's close
Flies the north wind laden with ambergris--
Oh, come to Shiraz when the north wind blows!
There abideth the angel Gabriel's peace
With him who is lord of its treasures; the fame
Of the sugar of Egypt shall fade and cease,
For the breath of our beauties has put it to shame.

Oh wind that blows from the sun-rising,
What news of the maid with the drunken eyes,
What news of the lovely maid dost thou bring?
Bid me not wake from my dream and arise,
In dreams I have rested my head at her feet--
When stillness unbroken around me lies,
The vision of her makes my solitude sweet.

If for wine the Cup-bearer pour forth my blood,
As the milk from a mother's bosom flows,
At his word let my heart yield its crimson flood.
But, Hafiz, Hafiz! thou art of those

For ever fearing lest absence be near;
For the days when thou held'st the Beloved close,
Why rise not thy thanks so that all may hear?

XXXI

THE breath of Dawn's musk-strewing wind shall blow,
The ancient world shall turn to youth again,
And other wines from out Spring's chalice flow;
Wine-red, the judas-tree shall set before
The pure white jessamine a brimming cup,
And wind flowers lift their scarlet chalice up
For the star-pale narcissus to adore.

The long-drawn tyranny of grief shall pass,
Parting shall end in meeting, the lament
Of the sad bird that sang "Alas, alas!"
Shall reach the rose in her red-curtained tent.
Forth from the mosque! the tavern calls to me!
Would'st hinder us? The preacher's homily
Is long, but life will soon be spent!

Ah, foolish Heart! the pleasures of To-day,
If thou abandon, will To-morrow stand
Thy surety for the gold thou'st thrown away?
In Sha'aban the troops of Grief disband,
And crown the hours with wine's red coronet--
The sun of merriment ere long will set,
And meagre Ramazan is close at hand!

Dear is the rose--now, now her sweets proclaim,
While yet the purple petals blush and blow;
Hither adown the path of Spring she came,
And by the path of Autumn she will go.
Now, while we listen, Minstrel, tune thy lay!
Thyself hast said: "The Present steals away

The Future comes, and bringing--what? Dost know?"

Summoned by thy melody did Hafiz rise
Out of the darkness near thy lips to dwell;
Back to the dark again his pathway lies--
Sing out, sing clear, and singing cry: Farewell!

XXXII

Upon a branch of the straight cypress-tree
Once more the patient nightingale doth rest:
"Oh Rose!" he cries, "evil be turned from thee!
I sing thee all men's thanks; thou blossomest
And hope springs up in every joyless heart--
Let not the nightingale lament apart,
Nor with thy proud thorns wound his faithful breast."

I will not mourn my woeful banishment,
He that has hungered for his lady's face
Shall, when she cometh, know a great content.
The Zealot seeks a heavenly dwelling-place,
Huris to welcome him in Paradise;
Here at the tavern gate my heaven lies,
I need no welcome but my lady's grace.

Better to drink red wine than tears, say I,
While the lute sings; and if one bid thee cease,
"God is the merciful!" thou shalt reply.
To some, life brings but joy and endless ease;
Ah, let them laugh although the jest be vain!
For me the source of pleasure lay in pain,
And weeping for my lady I found peace.

Hafiz, why art thou ever telling o'er
The tale of absence and of sorrow's night?
Knowest thou not that parting goes before
All meeting, and from darkness comes the light!

184

XXXIII

THE jewel of the secret treasury
Is still the same as once it was; the seal
Upon Love's treasure casket, and the key,
Are still what thieves can neither break nor steal;
Still among lovers loyalty is found,
And therefore faithful eyes still strew the ground
With the same pearls that mine once strewed for thee.

Question the wandering winds and thou shalt know
That from the dusk until the dawn doth break,
My consolation is that still they blow
The perfume of thy curls across my cheek.
A dart from thy bent brows has wounded me--
Ah, come! my heart still waiteth helplessly,
Has waited ever, till thou heal its pain.

If seekers after rubies there were none,
Still to the dark mines where the gems had lain
Would pierce, as he was wont, the radiant sun,
Setting the stones ablaze. Would'st hide the stain
Of my heart's blood? Blood-red the ruby glows
(And whence it came my wounded bosom knows)
Upon thy lips to show what thou hast done.

Let not thy curls waylay my pilgrim soul,
As robbers use, and plunder me no more!
Years join dead year, but thine extortionate rule
Is still the same, merciless as before.
Sing, Hafiz, sing again of eyes that weep!
For still the fountain of our tears is deep
As once it was, and still with tears is full.

XXXIV

Last night I dreamed that angels stood without
The tavern door, and knocked in vain, and wept;
They took the clay of Adam, and, methought,
Moulded a cup therewith while all men slept.
Oh dwellers in the halls of Chastity!
You brought Love's passionate red wine to me,
Down to the dust I am, your bright feet stept.

For Heaven's self was all too weak to bear
The burden of His love God laid on it,
He turned to seek a messenger elsewhere,
And in the Book of Fate my name was writ.
Between my Lord and me such concord lies.
As makes the Huris glad in Paradise,
With songs of praise through the green glades they flit.

A hundred dreams of Fancy's garnered store
Assail me--Father Adam went astray
Tempted by one poor grain of corn! Wherefore
Absolve and pardon him that turns away
Though the soft breath of Truth reaches his ears,
For two-and-seventy jangling creeds he hears,
And loud-voiced Fable calls him ceaselessly.

That, that is not the flame of Love's true fire
Which makes the torchlight shadows dance in rings,
But where the radiance draws the moth's desire
And send him forth with scorched and drooping wings.
The heart of one who dwells retired shall break,
Rememb'ring a black mole and a red cheek,
And his life ebb, sapped at its secret springs.

Yet since the earliest time that man has sought
To comb the locks of Speech, his goodly bride,
Not one, like Hafiz, from the face of Thought

186

Has torn the veil of Ignorance aside.

XXXV

Forget not when dear friend to friend returned,
Forget not days gone by, forget them not!
My mouth has tasted bitterness, and learned
To drink the envenomed cup of mortal lot;
Forget not when a sweeter draught was mine,
Loud rose the songs of them that drank that wine--
Forget them not!

Forget not loyal lovers long since dead,
Though faith and loyalty should be forgot,
Though the earth cover the enamoured head,
And in the dust wisdom and passion rot.
My friends have thrust me from their memory;
Vainly a thousand thousand times I cry:
Forget me not!

Weary I turn me to my bonds again.
Once there were hands strong to deliver me,
Forget not when they broke a poor slave's chain!
Though from mine eyes tears flow unceasingly,
I think on them whose rose gardens are set
Beside the Zindeh Rud, and I forget
Life's misery.

Sorrow has made her lair in my breast,
And undisturbed she lies--forget them not
That drove her forth like to a hunted beast!
Hafiz, thou and thy tears shall be forgot,
Lock fast the gates of thy sad heart! But those
That held the key to thine unspoken woes--
Forget them not!

XXXVI

Beloved, who has bid thee ask no more
How fares my life? to play the enemy
And ask not where he dwells that was thy friend?
Thou art the breath of mercy passing o'er
The whole wide world, and the offender I
Ah, let the rift my tears have channeled end,
Question the past no more!

If thou would'st know the secret of Love's fire,
It shall be manifest unto thine eyes:
Question the torch flame burning steadfastly,
But ask no more the sweet wind's wayward choir.
Ask me of faith and love that never dies;
Darius, Alexander's sovereignty,
I sing of these no more.

Ask not the monk to give thee Truth's pure gold,
He hides no riches 'neath his lying guise;
And ask not him to teach thee alchemy
Whose treasure-house is bare, his hearth-stone cold.
Ask to what goal the wandering dervish hies,
They knew not his desire who counselled thee:
Question his rags no more!

And in their learned books thou'lt seek in vain
The key to Love's locked gateway; Heart grown wise
In pain and sorrow, ask no remedy!
But when the time of roses comes again,
Take what it gives, oh Hafiz, ere it flies,
And ask not why the hour has brought it thee,
And wherefore ask no more!

XXXVII

ARISE! and fill a golden goblet up

188

Until the wine of pleasure overflow,
Before into thy skull's pale empty cup
A grimmer Cup-bearer the dust shall throw.
Yea, to the Vale of Silence we must come;
Yet shall the flagon laugh and Heaven's dome
Thrill with an answering echo ere we go!

Thou knowest that the riches of this field
Make no abiding, let the goblet's fire
Consume the fleeting harvest Earth may yield!
Oh Cypress-tree! green home of Love's sweet choir,
When I unto the dust I am have passed,
Forget thy former wantonness, and cast
Thy shadow o'er the dust of my desire.

Flow, bitter tears, and wash me clean! for they
Whose feet are set upon the road that lies
'Twixt Earth and Heaven Thou shalt be pure," they say,
"Before unto the pure thou lift thine eyes."
Seeing but himself, the Zealot sees but sin;
Grief to the mirror of his soul let in,
Oh Lord, and cloud it with the breath of sighs!

No tainted eye shall gaze upon her face,
No glass but that of an unsullied heart
Shall dare reflect my Lady's perfect grace.
Though like to snakes that from the herbage start,
Thy curling locks have wounded me full sore,
Thy red lips hold the power of the bezoar--
Ah, touch and heat me where I lie apart!

And when from her the wind blows perfume sweet,
Tear, Hafiz, like the rose, thy robe in two,
And cast thy rags beneath her flying feet,
To deck the place thy mistress passes through.

XXXVIII

I cease not from desire till my desire
Is satisfied; or let my mouth attain
My love's red mouth, or let my soul expire,
Sighed from those lips that sought her lips in vain.
Others may find another love as fair;
Upon her threshold I have laid my head,
The dust shall cover me, still lying there,
When from my body life and love have fled.

My soul is on my lips ready to fly,
But grief beats in my heart and will not cease,
Because not once, not once before I die,
Will her sweet lips give all my longing peace.
My breath is narrowed down to one long sigh
For a red mouth that burns my thoughts like fire;
When will that mouth draw near and make reply
To one whose life is straitened with desire?

When I am dead, open my grave and see
The cloud of smoke that rises round thy feet:
In my dead heart the fire still burns for thee;
Yea, the smoke rises from my winding-sheet!
Ah, come, Beloved! for the meadows wait
Thy coming, and the thorn bears flowers instead
Of thorns, the cypress fruit, and desolate
Bare winter from before thy steps has fled.

Hoping within some garden ground to find
A red rose soft and sweet as thy soft cheek,
Through every meadow blows the western wind,
Through every garden he is fain to seek.
Reveal thy face! that the whole world may be
Bewildered by thy radiant loveliness;
The cry of man and woman comes to thee,
Open thy lips and comfort their distress!

Each curling lock of thy luxuriant hair
Breaks into barbèd hooks to catch my heart,
My broken heart is wounded everywhere
With countless wounds from which the red drops start.
Yet when sad lovers meet and tell their sighs,
Not without praise shall Hafiz' name be said,
Not without tears, in those pale companies
Where joy has been forgot and hope has fled.

XXXIX

Cypress and Tulip and sweet Eglantine,
Of these the tale from lip to lip is sent;
Washed by three cups, oh Saki, of thy wine,
My song shall turn upon this argument.
Spring, bride of all the meadows, rises up,
Clothed in her ripest beauty: fill the cup!
Of Spring's handmaidens runs this song of mine.

The sugar-loving birds of distant Ind,
Except a Persian sweetmeat that was brought
To fair Bengal, have found nought to their mind.
See how my song, that in one night was wrought,
Defies the limits set by space and time!
O'er plains and mountain-tops my fearless rhyme,
Child of a night, its year-long road shall find.

And thou whose sense is dimmed with piety,
Thou too shalt learn the magic of her eyes;
Forth comes the caravan of sorcery
When from those gates the blue-veined curtains rise.
And when she walks the flowery meadows through,
Upon the jasmine's shamèd cheek the dew
Gathers like sweat, she is so fair to see!

Ah, swerve not from the path of righteousness
Though the world lure thee! like a wrinkled crone,
Hiding beneath her robe lasciviousness,
She plunders them that pause and heed her moan.
From Sinai Moses brings thee wealth untold;
Bow not thine head before the calf of gold
Like Samir, following after wickedness.

From the Shah's garden blows the wind of Spring,
The tulip in her lifted chalice bears
A dewy wine of Heaven's minist'ring
Until Ghiyasuddin, the Sultan, hears,
Sing, Hafiz, of thy longing for his face.
The breezes whispering round thy dwelling-place
Shall carry thy lament unto the King.

XL

THE margin of a stream, the willow's shade,
A mind inclined to song, a mistress sweet,
A Cup-bearer whose cheek outshines the rose,
A friend upon whose heart thy heart is laid:
Oh Happy-starred! let not thine hours fleet
Unvalued; may each minute as it goes
Lay tribute of enjoyment at thy feet,
That thou may'st live and know thy life is sweet.

Let every one upon whose heart desire
For a fair face lies like a burden sore,
That all his hopes may reach their goal unchecked,
Throw branches of wild rue upon his fire.
My soul is like a bride, with a rich store
Of maiden thoughts and jewelled fancies decked,
And in Time's gallery I yet may meet
Some picture meant for me, some image sweet.

Give thanks for nights spent in good company,

And take the gifts a tranquil mind may bring;
No heart is dark when the kind moon doth shine,
And grass-grown river-banks are fair to see.
The Saki's radiant eyes, God favouring,
Are like a wine-cup brimming o'er with wine,
And him my drunken sense goes out to greet,
For e'en the pain he leaves behind is sweet.

Hafiz, thy life has sped untouched by care,
With me towards the tavern turn thy feet!
The fairest robbers thou'lt encounter there,
And they will teach thee what to learn is sweet.

XLI

The days of Spring are here! the eglantine,
The rose, the tulip from the dust have risen--
And thou, why liest thou beneath the dust?
Like the full clouds of Spring, these eyes of mine
Shall scatter tears upon the grave thy prison,
Till thou too from the earth thine head shalt thrust.

XLII

TRUE love has vanished from every heart;
What has befallen all lovers fair?
When did the bonds of friendship part?--
What has befallen the friends that were?
Ah, why are the feet of Khizr lingering?--
The waters of life are no longer clear,
The purple rose has turned pale with fear,
And what has befallen the wind of Spring?

None now sayeth: "A love was mine,
Loyal and wise, to dispel my care."
None remembers love's right divine;

What has befallen all lovers fair?
In the midst of the field, to the players' feet,
The ball of God's favour and mercy came,
But none has leapt forth to renew the game--
What has befallen the horsemen fleet?

Roses have bloomed, yet no bird rejoiced,
No vibrating throat has rung with the tale;
What can have silenced the hundred-voiced?
What has befallen the nightingale?
Heaven's music is hushed, and the planets roll
In silence; has Zohra broken her lute?
There is none to press out the vine's ripe fruit,
And what has befallen the foaming bowl?

A city where kings are but lovers crowned,
A land from the dust of which friendship springs--
Who has laid waste that enchanted ground?
What has befallen the city of kings?
Years have passed since a ruby was won
From the mine of manhood; they labour in vain,
The fleet-footed wind and the quickening rain,
And what has befallen the light of the sun?
Hafiz, the secret of God's dread task
No man knoweth, in youth or prime
Or in wisest age; of whom would'st thou ask:
What has befallen the wheels of Time?

XLIII

Where are the tidings of union? that I may arise--
Forth from the dust I will rise up to welcome thee!
My soul, like a homing bird, yearning for Paradise,
Shall arise and soar, from the snares of the world set free.
When the voice of thy love shall call me to be thy slave,
I shall rise to a greater far than the mastery
Of life and the living, time and the mortal span:

Pour down, oh Lord! from the clouds of thy guiding grace.
The rain of a mercy that quickeneth on my grave,
Before, like dust that the wind bears from place to place,
I arise and flee beyond the knowledge of man.
When to my grave thou turnest thy blessed feet,
Wine and the lute thou shalt bring in thine hand to me,
Thy voice shall ring through the folds of my winding-sheet,
And I will arise and dance to thy minstrelsy.
Though I be old, clasp me one night to thy breast,
And I, when the dawn shall come to awaken me,
With the flush of youth on my check from thy bosom will rise.
Rise up! let mine eyes delight in thy stately grace!
Thou art the goal to which all men's endeavour has pressed,
And thou the idol of Hafiz' worship; thy face
From the world and life shall bid him come forth and arise!

Such passion and beauty can only be compared to the "Song of
Solomon."
3:1 On my bed by night
I sought him whom my soul loves;
   I sought him, but found him not.
2 I will rise now and go about the city,
   in the streets and in the squares;
I will seek him whom my soul loves.
   I sought him, but found him not.
3 The watchmen found me
   as they went about in the city.
"Have you seen him whom my soul loves?"

From Solomon to Rumi and Hafiz, the passion for the beloved
stays the same. In poetry and metaphor the seeker pours out
the contents of the heart, yearning, pleading, reaching, not only
for God, but for that eternal union, merging, oneness.

I am waiting for the guest. It is the longing that does the work.

Judaism and Jewish Mysticism

Scholars have long wondered why the God of the Old Testament had two names, El, usually translated as God, and Yahweh (Jehovah), usually translated as Lord. Moreover, the two deities seem to have different personalities.

The Canaanites, Eli, Il, or El was the supreme god, and the creator of all. El, or 'il-'ib was a general name for a deity, which may have been a god of the ancestors. As such, he was depicted as a grey or white haired, wise old man who guided his people. In the beginning, he was probably a desert god who, according to the older myths, had two wives and built a sanctuary with them and his new children in the desert. The idea of El having two wives shows up again in the Old Testament in a metaphorical story of El marrying Judah and Israel.

The close connection in the religions of the Canaanites and the Hebrews are notable. There are indications that the Hebrew people are an offshoot of the Canaanites. During the Egyptian rule of Canaan, it re-organized the territory. As a result, many people were left homeless and had to live in their caravans. Egyptians began calling them shashu "caravan people." The ancient Egyptian word for caravan people was similar to the word Hebrew. This is one of several theories but seems to be probable. Some scholars believe the term Hekw shashu (shepard kings) became the Greek word Hyksos which was used to refer to Jacob and his people when they settled in Lower Egypt. Remember that the titles of Jews or Israelites came from the name of the men Judah and Israel. Genisis 32:28

explains that God changed Jacob's name to Israel, which is why the Hebrews were also called Jacobites by some.

Three pantheon lists found at Ugarit begin with the four gods, El, Dagnu (the Dagon), and Ba'l'sapan, who was also called Hadad. Hadad was a storm god, whose other name was Ba'al.

Since El is a name for god in general, there would be names encountered such as Tôru El, or the Bull God. ("Bull El" or "the bull god"). Other names for El are bātnyu binwāti "Creator of creatures," 'abū banī 'ili "father of the gods," and 'abū 'adami "father of man." He is also called 'ēl 'ôlam "God Eternal."

Later, El would morph into a god of war, as the Jews would need such a deity in their conquests. Still, the compassionate face of the wise father god remained in the minds of the people and would be resurrected later in the New Testament.

According to the book, *"Canaanite Myth and Hebrew Epic; Essays in the History of the Religion of Israel,"* written by Frank Moore, published by Cambridge, Mass., Harvard University Press, 1973, and his book, *"From Epic to Canon: History and Literature in Ancient Israel"*, published by Johns Hopkins University press, c1998, Dr. Moore states in part:

"Religion, as a phenomenon of set rules and doctrine, was unknown and would be incomprehensible to the Canaanites and Israelites. Events transpired because the gods either willed it or did not oppose it. Plans and battles failed when the god opposed the plans or the planners, or if the gods were more inclined to the plan or persons of the enemies. Such beliefs saw the gods as fickle, arbitrary, and quixotic."

"In Syria-Palestine survival depended on the annual rains and rainfall varied widely from year to year. It was clear to Canaanites and Israelites that rainfall and thus crops were provided by the god whose powers included storms, rain, and fertility. This alone may be the answer to why the deity known as Ba'al remained in the Hebrew houses and temples for so long. Ba'al was the god of storms, and thus rain and crops."

"Unlike the people who valued the rains and crops above all, for a king it was important to have a god of power and war. El was such a god."

"El was a strong ruler and the divine warrior. We see El as the figure of the divine father. The one image of El that seems to run through all of his myths is that of the patriarch. Unlike the gods who represent the powers of nature (such as storms, rain, or procreation), El is the first social or family god. In the Akkadian, Amorite, and Canaanite religion, El frequently plays the role of "god of the father," who is fair, stern, and wise."
(End citation)

In a society built upon war and survival, the world and our view of God must have taken on a harsh tone. It is easy to assume that a male-driven theology would have only male attributes, and certainly, this monocular approach had its effect, but that is only part of the story. There is also the love prose of Solomon, and the passionate and flowing poetry of King David.

The chief god, El, and his wife, Ashtoreth, are said to have produced seventy divine children, some of whose names may be familiar, as they include Baal, Astarte, Anat, Resheph, the sun-goddess Shapshu, and the moon-god Yerak. Some sources also list the name, Yah, or Yahweh. These children came to be called, "the stars of El."

In the earliest stages of this religion, Yahweh appears to be simply one of these seventy children, each of whom was the patron deity of the seventy nations. We see this idea of city-state having patron gods brought into the ancient Greek religions as well. The idea also appears in the Dead Sea Scrolls reading and the Septuagint translation of Deuteronomy 32:8.

Deuteronomy 32:8-9
Douay-Rheims 1899 American Edition (DRA)
8) When the Most High divided the nations: when he separated the sons of Adam, he appointed the bounds of people according to the number of the children of Israel
9) And his people Jacob became the portion of the Lord, Israel was the line of his inheritance.

Some sources, including the Masoretic Text; Dead Sea Scrolls (see also Septuagint) renders "children of Israel" as "sons of God."

As the patriarch, El, had divided the land, each member of the divine family received a nation of his own: Israel is the portion of Yahweh. The statement, "according to the number of the children of Israel" has been translated by some as the children of god and is thought to include his seventy children.

Psalm 82 also presents the god, El, presiding over a divine assembly at which Yahweh stands up and makes his accusation against the other gods.

Psalm 82
Amplified Bible (AMP)
A Psalm of Asaph.
1) GOD stands in the assembly [of the representatives] of God; in the midst of the magistrates or judges He gives judgment [as] among the gods.
2) How long will you [magistrates or judges] judge unjustly and show partiality to the wicked? Selah [pause, and calmly think of that]!
3) Do justice to the weak (poor) and fatherless; maintain the rights of the afflicted and needy.

4) Deliver the poor and needy; rescue them out of the hand of the wicked.

5) [The magistrates and judges] know not, neither will they understand; they walk on in the darkness [of complacent satisfaction]; all the foundations of the earth [the fundamental principles upon which rests the administration of justice] are shaking.

6) I said, You are gods [since you judge on My behalf, as My representatives]; indeed, all of you are children of the Most High.

7) But you shall die as men and fall as one of the princes.

8) Arise, O God, judge the earth! For to You belong all the nations.

Thus was the beginning of the God of the Jews, Christians, and Muslims. But do not let the origin of any deity be of concern. Whether it is the thousand gods of the Hindu pantheon, the triune god of Christianity, Allah of Islam, or El of the Jews, all had a beginning in the minds and customs of man but all – every single deity and every concept of every deity - represents an aspect of the infinite truth captured and echoed in the heart of man as god revealed his/her nature.

Whether Yahweh was the son of El in the beginning of the mythos or not, at some time in the 8th century BCE, the names and deities begin to merge and be identified as one. Where El was a patriarchal and punitive God, Yahweh tended to interact with mankind. We see this merging in the story of Abraham, as he rejects his father's god and is called into communion with the "one true God." In Genesis 14, Abraham interacts with Melchizedek, a priest of El Elyon, and Abraham verbally equates Yahweh with El Elyon. Remember, as a rule, in the Bible "El" is translated as "God" (Elyon means the highest or the most high), and "Yahweh" is translated as "Lord."

It is within this final stage, yielding true monotheism, that god, El, and Yahweh merged. It is here that it could be said,

"Hear, O Israel: The LORD our God, the LORD is one."
Deut 6:4 New International Version

No matter how religion or the concept of God may have evolved, no matter the history or mingling of deity titles, names, or cultures, at the moment the seeker turns within, whether through meditation or examination, to find union and communion with the Beloved, all mystics become the same.

Genesis 14
Amplified Bible (AMP)
17) After his [Abram's] return from the defeat and slaying of Chedorlaomer and the kings who were with him, the king of Sodom went out to meet him at the Valley of Shaveh, that is, the King's Valley.

18) Melchizedek, king of Salem [later called Jerusalem] brought out bread and wine [for their nourishment]; he was the priest of God Most High,

19) And he blessed him and said, Blessed (favored with blessings, made blissful, joyful) be Abram by God Most High, Possessor and Maker of heaven and earth,

20) And blessed, praised, and glorified be God Most High, Who has given your foes into your hand! And [Abram] gave him a tenth of all [he had taken].

21) And the king of Sodom said to Abram, "Give me the persons and keep the goods for yourself."

22) But Abram said to the king of Sodom, "I have lifted up my hand and sworn to the Lord, God Most High, the Possessor, and Maker of heaven and earth,

23) That I would not take a thread or a shoelace or anything that is yours, lest you should say, I have made Abram rich."

According to the Old Testament book of Genesis in the Hebrew text, there was a balance of male and female forces within God from the beginning. Neither male nor female, both male and female, God showed the male energy of forming and shaping, as well as the female energy of nurturing and brooding. Although one may have a difficult time in distinguishing God the Spirit from the Spirit of God, according to Vine's Dictionary the word for "spirit" is "ruach" and is a female word.

Genesis 1
Amplified Bible
  1) In the beginning God (prepared, formed, fashioned, and) created the heavens and the earth.
  2) The earth was without form and an empty waste, and darkness was upon the face of the very great deep. The Spirit of God was moving (hovering, brooding) over the face of the waters.

The Holy Spirit is the designated representation of the feminine principle. This idea is supported by the Hebrew word for "spirit."

We shall see that the road within Jewish Mysticism is a search for esoteric and deepening knowledge. In it is a multitude of references to the soul, to union, the bride, the balance of male and female, the tripartite man and to creation. All of these religious ideas are aimed at knowing and experiencing God as deeply as possible for man to do. Jewish mysticism is different from other paths in that it is based on the pursuit of ever-deepening knowledge, which is applied to Kabbalah's Tree of Life. The Tree of Life is a general path that includes understanding, knowledge, wisdom, law, mercy, grace, and loving-kindness, to mention but a few of the steps.

There are three schools of Jewish Mysticism. Of these, Kabbalah is the most well known. Kabbalah emerged in 12th-century Europe and has continued to grow in popularity up to the present day. Among previous forms of mysticism to emerge were Merkabah mysticism (c.100 BCE – 1000 CE), and Chassidei Ashkenaz (early 1200s CE). Since Kabbalah is the most well known and practiced, and the other two disciplines have all but disappeared, we will focus primarily on Kabbalah.

Kabbalah means "received tradition", a term adopted to express their belief that they were not innovating, altering, or fabricating, but merely revealing the ancient hidden esoteric tradition within the Torah. This issue of whether Kabbalahists are discovering and revealing or simply fabricating, or worse yet, borrowing from occult sources rages until today. There are differing views on the origin of the Zohar, the main text of Kabbalah ranging from revelatory to occult.

The theosophical aspect of Kabbalah developed through two historical forms: "Medieval/Classic/Zoharic Kabbalah" (c.1175 – 1492 – 1570 CE), and Lurianic Kabbalah (1569 CE – today) which was built in part upon the ideas of Medieval Kabbalah. It is Lurianic Kabbalah that developed into the basis for modern Jewish Kabbalah.

Two new mystical forms of Kabbalah emerged after the Lurianic system. They are antinomian-heretical Sabbatean movements (1666 – 1700s CE), and Hasidic Judaism (1734 CE – today).

In contemporary Judaism, the only main forms of Jewish mysticism followed are esoteric Lurianic Kabbalah and its later commentaries, from various schools of Hasidic Judaism, and Neo-Hasidism and Neo-Kabbalah in non-Orthodox Jewish denominations.

The Kabbalistic form of Jewish mysticism itself divides into three general aims or goals: the Theosophical/Speculative Kabbalah seeks to understand and describe the divine realm, the Meditative/Ecstatic Kabbalah seeks to achieve a mystical union with God, and the Practical/Magical Kabbalah seeks to alter the world by altering divine realms. These three different, but inter-relating, methods or aims are found throughout Jewish mystical development and Kabbalah.

Kabbalah, literally is an esoteric method, discipline, and school of thought that originated in Judaism. A traditional Kabbalist in Judaism is called a Mekubbal.

Kabbalah's definition varies according to the tradition and aims of those following it, from its religious origin as an integral part of Judaism, to its later Christian, New Age, and Occultist amalgamation or attempted amalgamation of different religions, cultures, or schools. Kabbalah is a set of esoteric teachings meant to explain the relationship between an unchanging, eternal, and mysterious Ein Sof (infinity) and the mortal and finite universe (God's creation).

While it is heavily used by some denominations, it is not a religious denomination in itself. It forms the foundations of mystical religious interpretation. It also presents methods to aid understanding of the concepts and thereby attain spiritual realization.

Kabbalah was originally developed entirely within the realm of Jewish thought, and kabbalists often use classical Jewish sources to explain and demonstrate its esoteric teachings. These teachings are held by followers in Judaism to define the inner meaning of both the Hebrew Bible and traditional Rabbinic literature and their formerly concealed transmitted dimension, as well as to explain the significance of Jewish religious observances.

Historically, Kabbalah emerged, after earlier forms of Jewish mysticism, in 12th- to 13th-century Southern France and Spain. It is interesting to note that Tarot Cards originated in the same period of time in Italy and show some influence of Kabbalah. Kabbalah evolved after being reinterpreted in the Jewish mystical renaissance of 16th-century Ottoman Palestine

Modern Kabbalah was popularized in the form of Hasidic Judaism from the 18th century onwards. In the 19th century onward there have been various combinations of Kabbalah and other spiritual and occult sources.

According to the Zohar, a foundational text of Kabbalah, Torah study can proceed along four levels of interpretation (exegesis). These four levels are called pardes from their initial letters, which in Hebrew mean "orchard".

Peshat: "simple" - the direct interpretations of meaning.
Remez: "hints" - the allegoric meanings through allusion with Torah.
Derash: "inquire" or "seek" - midrashic (Rabbinic) meanings, often with imaginative comparisons with similar words or verses.
Sod: "secret" or "mystery" - the inner, esoteric or metaphysical meanings, expressed in Kabbalah.

For allusions to be used the initiate would be at the mercy of the teacher since allusion may be drawn, with some convolutions, between any number of passages. Likewise, for secret teaching to be used there are no safeguards to keep the teachings pure and true since by nature, no one but the teacher knows the secrets.

The above reasons may be why Kabbalah teaches doctrines that are accepted by some Jews as the true meaning of Judaism while other Jews have rejected these doctrines as heretical and antithetical to Judaism.

The Theosophical or Theoretical Kabbalah is from the Luria school of Kabbalah and uses the Zohar extensively and seeks to understand and describe the divine realm and its relationship to mankind. By understanding the divine realm Jewish mysticism strives to achieve a mystical union with God.

Although the evolution of Kabbalah into some of its modern forms has borrowed from various occult schools, ancient systems seemed to stay focused on the mystical journey by attempting to understand the spiritual nature of God and man.

Merkabah/Merkavah mysticism (or Chariot mysticism) is a school of early Jewish mysticism, c. 100 BCE – 1000 CE, centered on visions such as those found in the Book of Ezekiel chapter 1, or in the hekhalot ("palaces") literature, concerning stories of ascents to the heavenly palaces and the Throne of God. The main corpus of the Merkabah literature was composed in Israel in the period 200–700 CE, although later references to the Chariot tradition can also be found in the literature of the Chassidei Ashkenaz in the Middle Ages.

A major text in this tradition is the Maaseh Merkabah (Works of the Chariot). Merkabah means, "a thing to ride" or chariot." The word "chariot" is found 44 times in the Masoretic text of the Hebrew Bible – most of them referring to normal chariots on earth, and although the concept of the Merkabah is associated with Ezekiel's vision (1:4–26), the word is not explicitly written in Ezekiel 1. However, when left untranslated, in English the Hebrew term merkabah relates to the throne-chariot of God in prophetic visions and of the four-wheeled vehicle driven by four hayyot ("living creatures"), each of which has four wings and the four faces of a man, lion, ox, and eagle (or vulture).

The Chariot, palaces, or ascension schools also draw heavily from the Books of Enoch. More information on the books of 1 Enoch, 2 Enoch, and 3 Enoch may be found through Fifth Estate Publishing.

This type of literature and Kabbalic thought has evolved through four stages.

800–500 BC, mystical elements in Prophetic Judaism such as Ezekiel's chariot

Beginning c.530s BC, especially 300–100 BC, Apocalyptic literature mysticism

Beginning c.100 BC, especially 1-130s CE, early Rabbinic Merkabah mysticism referred to briefly in exoteric Rabbinic literature such as the Pardes ascent; also related to early Christian mysticism

c.1–200 CE, continuing till c.1000 CE, merkabah mystical ascent accounts in the esoteric Merkabah-Hekhalot literature.

To most Jews the idea of actually being able to see and perceive God is not only inconceivable but also blasphemous. It is believed that any description portrays God's created glory. The glory was not created by God, but emanated from God in a similar manner to the way that light emanates from the sun. This glory is manifested as his messenger, his exalted angel, created to give the prophets something concrete to visualize.

What emerged for the Hasidei Ashkenaz is a tripartite system composed of God, the higher Kavod, and the lower Kavod - (Kavod – honor, power). God is beyond human comprehension and impossible for man to sense or comprehend. The higher Kavod emanates from God and is still very distant from man, but slightly more accessible. And finally, the lower Kavod is the element that man can access. It is at the lower Kavod that man can attempt to understand.

This description of God and His divine realm directly parallels the kabbalistic ten-headed, ten stages or ten element sefirotic system. In this system the top element, Ein Sof, is beyond knowledge and is impossible for man to reach or understand. The elements emanate downward. The lower the sefira, the more access man has. The lower Kavod is not separate from the higher Kavod but instead emanates from it. It is the lower emanations from God that man begins to apprehend and from there he attempts to reach higher and higher toward God and the mystic's understanding. With each step the mystic is changed spiritually and with each spiritual change higher lessons are learned and the deeper his relationship with God.

Kabbalah seeks God through study, research, and the deepening accumulation of knowledge, which brings wisdom, which brings growth, which brings closeness to God.

Some Thought From Jewish Mystics

"Just as the soul fills the body, so God fills the world. Just as the soul bears the body, so God endures the world. Just as the soul sees but is not seen, so God sees but is not seen. Just as the soul feeds the body spiritually and intellectually, so God gives food to the world" (T.B. Berachoth, 10a)

There was originally one 'Universal Soul,' or 'Over-soul,' which, as it were, broke itself up and encased itself in individual bodies. All individual souls are, hence, fragments of the 'Oversoul,' so that although they are distinct from one another they are, in reality, all one. Thus, to quote the Zohar:

"At the time when God desired to create the universe, it came up in His will before Him, and He formed all the souls which were destined to be allotted to the children of men. The souls were all before Him in the forms which they were afterwards destined to bear inside the human body. God looked at each one of them, and He saw that many of them would act corruptly in the world. When the time of each arrived, it was summoned before God, who said to it: 'Go to such and such a part of the universe, enclose thyself in such and such a body.' But the soul replied: 'O sovereign of the universe, I am happy in my present world, and I desire not to leave it for some other place where I shall be enslaved and become soiled.' Then the Holy One (blessed be He) replied: 'From the day of thy creation thou hast had no other destiny than to go into the universe whither I send thee.' The soul, seeing that it must obey, sorrowfully took the way to earth and came down to dwell in our midst" (ii. 96).

"The lower soul desires a body and lives in the stage of sense... The higher soul, on the other hand, transcends the body, 'rides upon it,' as the fish is in the sea or as the plant is in the air. This higher soul never absolutely leaves its home, its being is not here but 'yonder,' or, in the language of Plotinus, 'The soul always leaves something of itself above'" (Rufus M. Jones, Studies in Mystical Religion, p. 74). This is the same idea of the body and soul being separate.

The soul is a trinity. "In these three of Neshāmāh, Ruaḥ, Nefesh (nefesh – instinctual soul, ruach – emotional soul, neshamah – intellectual soul) we find an exact image (diyūkna) of what is above in the celestial world. For all three form only one soul, one being, where all is one. The Nefesh [i.e. the lowest side of soul] does not in itself possess any light. This is why it is so tightly joined to the body, acquiring for it the pleasures and the foods which it needs. It is of it that the sage says, 'She giveth meat to her household and their task to her maidens' (Proverbs, xxxi. 15). 'Her household' means the body which is fed. 'Her maidens' are the limbs which obey the dictates of the body. Above the Nefesh is the Ruaḥ [the ethical soul] which dominates the Nefesh, imposes laws upon it and enlightens it as much as its nature requires. And then high above the Ruaḥ is the Neshāmāh, which in its turn rules the Ruaḥ and sheds upon it the light of life. The Ruaḥ is lit up by this light, and depends entirely upon it. After death, the Ruaḥ has no rest. The gates of Paradise (Eden) are not opened to it until the time when Neshāmāh has reascended to its source, to the Ancient of the ancients, in order to become filled with Him throughout eternity.

"If thou inquirest why it [i.e.. the soul] cometh down into the world from so exalted a place and putteth itself at such a distance from its source, I reply thus: It may be likened to an earthly monarch to whom a son is born. The monarch takes the son to the countryside, there to be nourished and trained until such a time as he is old enough to accustom himself to the palace of his father. When the father is told that the education of his son is completed, what does he do out of his love for him? In order to celebrate his home-coming, he sends for the queen, the mother of the lad. He brings her into the palace and rejoices with her the whole day long.

"It is thus with the Holy One (blessed be He). He, too, has a son by the queen. This son is the high and holy soul. He conducts it to the countryside, i.e. to the world, in order to grow up there and gain an acquaintance with the customs appertaining to the royal palace. When the Divine King perceives that the soul has completed its growth, and the time is ripe for recalling it to Himself, what does He do out of His love for it? He sends for the queen, brings her into the palace, and brings the soul in too. The soul, forsooth, does not bid adieu to its earthly tenement before the queen has come to unite herself with it, and to lead it into the royal apartment where it is to live for ever."

"And the people of the world are wont to weep when the son [i.e. the soul] takes its leave of them. But if there be a wise man amongst them, he says to them, Why weep ye? Is he not the son of the King? Is it not meet that he should take leave of you to live in the palace of his father? It was for this reason that Moses, who knew the Truth, on seeing the inhabitants of earth mourning for the dead, exclaimed, 'Ye are the children of the Lord your God; ye shall not cut yourselves, nor make any baldness between your eyes for the dead' (Deut. xiv. 1). If all

210

good men knew this, they would hail with delight the day when it behoves them to bid adieu to the world. Is it not the height of glory for them when the queen [i.e. the Shechinah, the Divine Presence] comes down into the midst of them to lead them into the palace of the king to enjoy the delights thereof for ever-more?" (i. 245).

"At the moment when the earthly union [i.e. marriage] takes place, the Holy One (blessed be He) sends to earth a form [or image] resembling a man, and bearing upon itself the divine seal. This image is present at the moment just mentioned, and if the eye could see what goes on then, it would detect above the heads [of man and wife] an image like a human face, and this image is the model after which we are fashioned. . . . It is this image which receives us first on our arrival into this world. It grows in us as we grow, and leaves us when we leave the world. This image is from above. When the souls are about to quit their heavenly abode each soul appears before the Holy One (blessed be He) clothed with an exalted pattern [or image or form] on which are engraven the features which it will bear here below" (iii. 107).

"Whosoever serves God out of love," says the Zohar, "comes into union (itdabak) with the place of the Highest of the High, and comes into union, too, with the holiness of the world which is to be" (ii. 216).

"Come and see! When the souls have reached the treasury of life they enjoy the shining of the brilliant mirror whose focus is in the heavens. And such is the brightness which emanates therefrom that the souls would be unable to withstand it, were they not covered with a coat of light. Even Moses could not approach it until he had stripped off his earthly integument" (i. 66). Again: "In one of the most mysterious and exalted parts of heaven, there is a palace called the Palace of Love. Deep mysteries are enacted there; there are gathered together all the most well-beloved souls of the Heavenly King; it is there that the Heavenly King, the Holy One (blessed be He), lives together with these holy souls and unites Himself to them by kisses of love" (ii. 97).

"When Adam our first father dwelt in the garden of Eden he was clothed, as men are in heaven, with the Divine light. When he was driven forth from Eden to do the ordinary work of earth, then Holy Writ tells us that 'the Lord God made for Adam and for his wife coats of skin and clothed them.' For, ere this, they wore coats of light, of that light which belongs to Eden. 1 Man's good deeds upon earth bring down on him a portion of the higher light which lights up heaven. It is that light which covers him like a coat when he enters into the future world and appears before his Maker, the Holy One (blessed be He). It is by means of such a covering that he can taste of the enjoyments of the elect and look upon the face of the 'shining mirror.' And thus, the soul, in order to become perfect in all respects, must have a different covering for each of the two worlds which it has to inhabit, one for the terrestrial world and the other for the higher world" (ii. 229).

"Before having created any shape in the world, before having produced any form, He was alone, without form, resembling nothing. Who could comprehend Him as He then was, before creation, since He had no form? It is forbidden to picture Him by any form or under any shape whatsoever, not even by His holy name, nor by a letter [of the alphabet] nor by a point [the Yod, which is the smallest letter. Such is the sense of the words, 'For ye saw no manner of similitude on the day when the Lord spake unto you in Horeb, out of the midst of the fire' (Deut. iv. 15).

You cannot tell what God is; you can only tell what He is not. "Believe not that man consists solely of flesh, skin, bones, and veins. The real part of man is his soul, and the things just mentioned, the skin, flesh, bones, and veins, are only an outward covering, a veil, but are not the man. When man departs he divests himself of all the veils which cover him. And these different parts of our body correspond to the secrets of the Divine wisdom. The skin typifies the heavens which extend everywhere and cover everything like a garment. The flesh puts us in mind of the evil side of the universe. The bones and the veins symbolise the Divine chariot, the inner powers of man which are the servants of God. But they are all but an outer covering. For, inside man, there is the secret of the Heavenly Man. . . . Everything below takes place in the same manner as everything above. This is the meaning of the remark that God created man in His own image. But just as in the heavens, which cover the whole universe, we behold different shapes brought about by the stars and the planets to teach us concerning hidden things and deep secrets, so upon the skin which covers our body there are shapes and forms which are like planets and stars to our bodies. All these shapes have a hidden meaning, and are observed by the sages who are able to read the face of man" (ii. 76a).

The idea expressed in just the last paragraph expresses parallel thoughts of the Christian mystic who wrote, "The Cloud of Unknowing" and also to that basic teaching of Zen Buddhism to forget everything that exists in our mind, for we think only of that which is created materially and mentally. Anything we can conceive or perceive is not God. Eliminate them all and only God remains.

"Believe not that man consists solely of flesh, skin, bones, and veins. The real part of man is his soul, and the things just mentioned, the skin, flesh, bones, and veins, are only an outward covering, a veil, but are not the man. When man departs he divests himself of all the veils which cover him. "

"That in the time of this word all the creatures that ever have
been, be now, or ever shall be, and all the works of those same
creatures, should be hid under the cloud of forgetting...
Yea! and, if it be courteous and seemly to say, in this work it
profiteth little or nought to think of the kindness or the
worthiness of God, nor on our Lady, nor on the saints or
angels in heaven, nor yet on the joys in heaven: that is to say,
with a special beholding to them, as thou wouldest by that
beholding feed and increase thy purpose. I trow that on
nowise it should help in this case and in this work. For
although it be good to think upon the kindness of God, and to
love Him and praise Him for it, yet it is far better to think
upon the naked being of Him, and to love Him and praise
Him for Himself."
The Cloud of Unknowing, ed. by Evelyn Underhill, [1922] Pg. 88

Of the Zen practice of sitting and forgetting called "Zazen" –
meditation, is it said:
"I'm making progress," said Yen Hui.
"What do you mean?" asked Confucius.
"I have forgotten rites and music."
"Not bad, but you still haven't got it."
Yen Hui saw Confucius again on another day and said, "I'm
making progress."
"What do you mean?"
"I have forgotten humaneness and righteousness."
"Not bad, but you still haven't got it."
Yen Hui saw Confucius again on another day and said, "I'm
making progress."
"What do you mean?"
"I sit and forget."
"What do you mean, 'sit and forget'?" Confucius asked with
surprise.
"I slough off my limbs and trunk," said Yen Hui, "dim my
intelligence, depart from my form, leave knowledge behind,

and become identical with the Transformational Thoroughfare. This is what I mean by 'sit and forget'."

Jewish mystics knew the soul is not the body, but the body is a simple vessel. The soul fills the body and God fills the world. We cannot know God. We cannot picture God. We can only know what He is not. Put all that he is not out of mind and what is left is God. He is the universal soul. In the beginning there was one universal soul. We came from that soul and to it we will return. This returning is the blessed marriage spoken of in the Jewish texts. How these words echo mystics of other paths.

Hinduism, Gurus and Swamis

Hinduism denotes a wide variety of related religious traditions native to South Asia notably in Nepal and India. Its history overlaps or coincides with the development of religion in Indian subcontinent since the Iron Age, with some of its traditions tracing back to prehistoric religions such as those of the Bronze Age Indus Valley Civilization. It has thus been called the "oldest religion" in the world.

Scholars regard Hinduism as a synthesis of various Indian cultures and traditions, with diverse roots and no single founder.

The history of Hinduism is often divided into periods of development, with the first period being that of the Historical Vedic Religion dated from about 1750 BCE.

The subsequent period, between 800 BCE and 200 BCE, is "a turning point between the Vedic religion and Hindu religions", and a formative period for Hinduism, Jainism and Buddhism.

The Epic and Early Puranic period, from c. 200 BCE to 500 CE, saw the classical "Golden Age" of Hinduism, which coincides with the Gupta Empire. In this period the six branches of Hindu philosophy evolved, namely Samkhya, Yoga, Nyaya, Vaisheshika, Mimamsa, and Vedanta. Monotheistic sects like Shaivism and Vaishnavism developed during this same period through the Bhakti movement.

Bhakti means "attachment, participation, devotion to, fondness for, homage, faith or love, worship, piety to (as a religious principle or means of salvation)".

Bhakti, in Hinduism, refers to devotion and the love of a personal god or a representational god by a devotee. Bhakti is a path of love, devotion, and service toward God for its own purpose, not wanting or expecting divine reward. It is the path of love leading to union with God.

In ancient texts such as the Shvetashvatara Upanishad, the term simply means participation in, devotion and love for any endeavor, or it refers to one of the possible paths of spirituality and moksha as in bhakti marga mentioned in the Bhagavad Gita. It is in the Upanishad that the idea of karma is introduced. This is similar to the Christian idea of sowing what one reaps but carried over multiple lifetimes via reincarnation.

The term also refers to a movement that arose between the 7th century and 10th century CE in India, focussed on the gods Vishnu and Shiva, possibly in response to the arrival of Islam in India.

The Bhakti movement reached North India in the Delhi Sultanate. It grew throughout the Mughal era evolving into Hinduism as we recognize it today. When Muslims conquered the religion the general population was allowed to live as Dhimmi. (Dhimmi is a person living in an area which was overrun or conquered by Islam but was allowed to keep his or her original faith if they pay a tax and follow certain rules.)

Bhakti-like movements also spread to other Indian religions during this period, and it influenced the interaction between Christianity and Hinduism in the modern era.

The Bhakti movement rose in importance during the medieval history of Hinduism, starting with Southern India with the Vaisnava Alvars and Shaiva Nayanars, growing rapidly therefrom with the spread of Bhakti poetry and devotion throughout India by the 12th-18th century CE.

The Bhagavata Purana is a text associated with the Bhakti movement which elaborates the concept of bhakti as found in the Bhagavad Gita.

The Bhagavad Gita lit. "Song of the Lord", referred to as simply the Gita, is a 700-verse Hindu scripture in Sanskrit that is part of the Hindu epic Mahabharata.

The Gita is set in a narrative framework of a dialogue between Pandava prince Arjuna and his guide and charioteer Krishna as they faced their duties as warriors. Part of the dialogue in the Gita is between diverging attitudes concerning and methods toward the attainment of liberation.

Dharma in Hinduism differs from the way the word is used in Zen. Hinduism accepts the concept of reincarnation, and what determines the state of an individual in the next existence is karma, which refers to the actions undertaken by the body and the mind. In order to achieve good karma it is important to live life according to dharma or what is right. This involves doing what is right for the individual, the family, the class or caste and also for the universe itself. Dharma is like a cosmic norm and if one goes against the norm it can result in bad karma. So, dharma affects the future according to the karma accumulated. Therefore one's dharmic path in the next life is the one necessary to bring to fruition all the results of past karma.

The Bhagavad Gita presents a synthesis of the Brahmanical concept of dharma, theistic bhakti, the yogic ideals of the transcendental state of liberation through jnana, bhakti, karma, and raja yoga (spoken of in the 6th chapter) and Samkhya philosophy.

Guru is a Sanskrit term for "teacher" or "master", particularly in Indian religions. The Hindu guru-shishya tradition is the oral tradition or religious doctrine or experiential wisdom

218

transmitted from teacher to student. In the United States, the word guru is a newer term, most often used to describe a teacher from the Hindu tradition. In the West some derogatory interpretations of the word have been noted, reflecting certain gurus who have allegedly exploited their followers' naiveté, due to the use of the term in certain new religious movements.

Guru in Hinduism

The importance of finding a guru who can impart transcendental knowledge (vidyā) is emphasized in Hinduism. The Bhagavad Gita, is a dialogue between God in the form of Krishna and his friend Arjuna, a Kshatriya prince who accepts Krishna as his guru on the battlefield, prior to a large battle. Not only does this dialogue outline many of the ideals of Hinduism, but their relationship is considered an ideal one of Guru-Shishya(student-teacher). In the Gita, Krishna speaks to Arjuna of the importance of finding a guru:

"Acquire the transcendental knowledge from a Self-realized master by humble reverence, by sincere inquiry, and by service. The wise ones who have realized the Truth will impart the Knowledge to you."

In the sentence mentioned above, guru is used more or less interchangeably with satguru (literally: true teacher), paratpar Guru and satpurusha.

The role of the guru continues in the original sense of the word in such Hindu traditions as the Vedānta, Yoga, Tantra and Bhakti schools. Indeed, it is now a standard part of Hinduism that a guru is one's spiritual guide on earth. In some more mystical traditions it is believed that the guru could awaken dormant spiritual knowledge within the pupil. The act of doing this is known as shaktipat.

In Hinduism, the guru is considered a respected person with saintly qualities who enlightens the mind of his or her disciple, an educator from whom one receives the initiatory mantra, and one who instructs in rituals and religious ceremonies. A mantra is a series of words or sounds that is used to clear and focus the mind. Hindu texts regard the teacher and the mother and father as the most venerable influences on an individual.

The guru-shishya tradition is the transmission of teachings from a guru (teacher to a 'śiṣya' (disciple). In this relationship, subtle and advanced knowledge is conveyed and received through the student's respect, commitment, devotion and obedience. The student eventually masters the knowledge that the guru embodies.

In Indian culture, a person without a guru, or a teacher (acharya), was once looked down on as an orphan, or unfortunate person. A guru also gives spiritual awakening of the disciple by the grace of the guru. Diksha is also considered to be the procedure of bestowing the divine powers of a guru upon the disciple, through which the disciple progresses continuously along the path to divinity.

Grace is a universal concept running through most religions. It is the doorway to the mystical path. The universe, God, or his representative such as a messiah or a guru gives us grace. It is unmerited favor that opens the heart and lets us transcend.

The concept of the "guru" can be traced back as far as the early Upanishads, when the idea of the Divine Teacher on earth first manifested from its early Brahmin associations.
This is called the guru-shishya tradition.
Adi Shankara with Disciples, by Raja Ravi Varma (1904)

The dialogue between guru and disciple is a fundamental component of Hinduism, established in the oral traditions of the Upanishads (c. 2000 BC). The term Upanishad derives from the Sanskrit words upa (near), ni (down) and ṣad (to sit) — "sitting down near" a spiritual teacher to receive instruction. In the Upanishads, the guru-disciple relationship appears in many settings (a husband answers a wife's questions about immortality; a teenage boy is taught by Yama, who is Death personified, etc.) Sometimes the sages are female, and sometimes the instruction is sought by kings.

The title of Swami means, "master" and refers to male Hindu teachers. Swami is the human incarnation of the Lord. Swami can also be a Guru. A Guru is a human being who preaches the knowledge, which was already preached by the Lord. Hindus see no contradiction of having many swamis or incarnations of the Lord at the same time. It would be compared to the Christian concept of the Spirit of God inhabiting more than one believer at a time.

We will now explore the wisdom of Hinduism in the following passages:

...O Nanak a truly religious leader should be known as such only if he brings all people together...
- Guru Granth Sahib

...All have equal rights in affairs. Nobody is an outsider...
- Guru Granth Sahib

...Everybody is my friend and I am a friend of everybody...
- Guru Granth Sahib

...The world is going up in flames O Lord— shower it with Your Mercy, Save it, and deliver it from sin through whichever door (religion) humanity approaches...
- Guru Granth Sahib

...Hinduism may not be my faith, and I may believe not in the supremacy of Veda or the Brahmins, nor in idol worship or caste or pilgrimages and other rituals, but I would fight for the right of all Hindus to live with honour and practice their faith according to their own rites...For me, there is only one religion – of God – and whosoever belongs to it, be he a Hindu or a Muslim, him I own and he owns me. I neither convert others by force, nor submit to force, to change my faith...
- Guru Tegh Bahadur

...There is a garden, in which so many plants have grown. They bear the Ambrosial Nectar of the Naam [Name of God] as their fruit. Consider this, O wise one, by which you may attain the state of Nirvaanaa. All around this garden are pools of poison, but within it is the Ambrosial Nectar, O Siblings of Destiny. There is only one gardener who tends it. He takes care of every leaf and branch. He brings all sorts of plants and plants them there. They all bear fruit - none is without fruit.
- (Guru Arjan, Asa, pg. 385)

...The temple or the mosque are the same, the Hindu worship or the Musalman prayer are the same; all men are the same; it is through error they appear different. Deities, demons, Yakshas, heavenly singers, Musalmans and Hindus adopt the customary dress of their different countries. All men have the same eyes, the same ears, the same body, the same build, a compound of earth, air, fire, and water. Allah and Abhekh are the same, the Purans and the Quran are the same; they are all alike; it is the one God who created all. The Hindu God and the Muhammadan God are the same; let no man even by mistake suppose there is a difference.
- (Guru Gobind Singh, Akal Ustat, pg. 275)

Blessed is the place, and blessed are those who dwell there, where God's Name is meditated upon. The sermons and songs

of God's praises are sung there and there is nothing but peace, poise and tranquillity.
- (Guru Arjan, Raga Bilaval, pg. 816)

If the Lord Allah lives only in the mosque, then to whom does the rest of the world belong? ...The God of the Hindus lives in the southern lands, and the God of the Muslims lives in the west. So search in your heart - look deep into your heart of hearts; this is the home and the place where God lives.
- (Bhagat Kabir, pg. 1349)

Sikhism was the first religion to proclaim in its scriptures the full, unequivocal and complete equality between men and women in all spheres/aspects of life, including the religious life. In this respect the Sikh Gurus, beginning with Nanak in the fifteenth century, advocated and encouraged a radical, innovative and revolutionary social egalitarianism that was far ahead of its time.

We are born of woman, we are conceived in the womb of woman, we are engaged and married to woman. We make friendship with woman and the lineage continued because of woman. When one woman dies, we take another one, we are bound with the world through woman. Why should we talk ill of her, who gives birth to kings? The woman is born from woman; there is none without her. Only the One True Lord is without woman
- (Guru Nanak, Var Asa, pg. 473)

To this end, Sikhism does not believe in women wearing veils. Stay, stay, O daughter-in-law - do not cover your face with a veil. In the end, this shall not bring you even half a shell.
- (Bhagat Kabir, Asa, pg. 484)

There is but One God, His name is Truth, He is the Creator, He fears none, he is without hate, He never dies, He is beyond

the cycle of births and death, He is self illuminated, He is realized by the kindness of the True Guru. He was True in the beginning, He was True when the ages commenced and has ever been True, He is also True now.
Guru Nanak quotes (Indian Spiritual leader, 1469-1539)

The biggest guru-mantra is: Never share your secrets with anybody. It will destroy you.
Chanakya quotes (Indian Politician, strategist and Writer, 350 BC-275 BC

The great secret of true success, of true happiness, is this: the man or woman who asks for no return, the perfectly unselfish person, is the most successful.
-Swami Vivekananda

Put your heart, mind, and soul into even your smallest acts. This is the secret of success.
-Swami Sivananda

A grain of devotion is more valuable than tons of faithlessness.
-A.C. Bhaktivedanta Swami Prabhupada

One should not be happy or distressed over desirables and undesirables, knowing that such feelings are just created by the mind.
-A.C. Bhaktivedanta Swami Prabhupada

Your duty is to treat everybody with love as a manifestation of the Lord.
-Swami Sivananda

A spiritually illumined soul lives in the world, yet is never contaminated by it.
-Swami Bhaskarananda

All differences in this world are of degree, and not of kind, because oneness is the secret of everything.
-Swami Vivekananda

Serve your True Lord and Master, and you shall be blessed with true greatness. By Guru's Grace, He abides in the mind, and egotism is driven out. This wandering mind comes to rest, when the Lord casts His Glance of Grace.
Sri Guru Granth Sahib quotes

I am egotistical and conceited, and my intellect is ignorant. Meeting the Guru, my selfishness and conceit have been abolished. The illness of egotism is gone, and I have found peace.
Sri Guru Granth Sahib quotes

Meeting the True One, Truth wells up. The truthful are absorbed into the True Lord. Intuitive understanding is obtained and one is welcomed with honor, through the Guru's Word, filled with the Fear of God. O Nanak, the True King absorbs us into Himself.
Sri Guru Granth Sahib quotes

Let no man in the world live in delusion. Without a Guru none can cross over to the other shore.
Guru Nanak quotes (Indian Spiritual leader, 1469-1539)

Serving the True Guru, I have found the Treasure of Excellence. Its value cannot be estimated.
Sri Guru Granth Sahib quotes

Through the Guru's Teachings, it is revealed. Meeting with the True One, peace is found.
Sri Guru Granth Sahib quotes

My condition, O my True Guru - that condition, O Lord, is
known only to You. I was rolling around in the dirt, and no one
cared for me at all.
Sri Guru Granth Sahib quotes

Blessed is the mother who gave birth; blessed and respected
is the father of one who serves the True Guru and finds peace.
His arrogant pride is banished from within. Standing at the
Lord's Door, the humble Saints serve Him; they find the
Treasure of Excellence.
Sri Guru Granth Sahib quotes

By Guru's Grace, a few come to understand; they center their
consciousness in the fourth state.
Sri Guru Granth Sahib quotes

When the Dear Lord grants His Forgiveness, this human
body finds lasting peace. By Guru's Grace, I serve the True
One, who is Immeasurably Deep and Profound.
Sri Guru Granth Sahib quotes

O Siblings of Destiny, those who lack devotion - why have
they even bothered to come into the world? They do not serve
the Perfect Guru; they waste away their lives in vain.
Sri Guru Granth Sahib quotes

The Guru is the Ladder, the Guru is the Boat, and the Guru
is the Raft to take me to the Lord's Name. The Guru is the Boat
to carry me across the world-ocean; the Guru is the Sacred
Shrine of Pilgrimage, the Guru is the Holy River. If it pleases
Him, I bathe in the Pool of Truth, and become radiant and
pure.
Sri Guru Granth Sahib quotes

By actions committed under the influence of the three
qualities, hope and anxiety are produced. Without the Guru,
how can anyone be released from these three qualities?

Through intuitive wisdom, we meet with Him and find peace. Within the home of the self, the Mansion of His Presence is realized when He bestows His Glance of Grace and washes away our pollution.
Sri Guru Granth Sahib quotes

By Guru's Grace, I have found Him within the home of my own heart. I serve Him constantly, and I meditate on Him single-mindedly.
Sri Guru Granth Sahib quotes

Hagar: What is the key to happiness? Guru: Abstinence, poverty, fasting, and celibacy

Through the Guru's Teachings, I merge with intuitive ease into the Lord, the Life of the World, the Fearless One, the Great Giver.
Sri Guru Granth Sahib quotes

By Guru's Grace, intuitive understanding is obtained; subduing the sense of duality, they are in love with the One.
Sri Guru Granth Sahib quotes

I have quit searching outside; the Guru has shown me that God is within the home of my own heart.
Sri Guru Granth Sahib quotes

when the Guru drives out doubt, then the soul-bride enters the Mansion of the Lord's Presence.
Sri Guru Granth Sahib quotes

The angelic beings and the silent sages long for Him; the True Guru has given me this understanding.
Sri Guru Granth Sahib quotes

Meeting with the Guru, intuitive balance is obtained, when God, in His Will, grants His Grace.
Sri Guru Granth Sahib quotes

Emotional attachment to Maya is shed with intuitive ease, through the Guru's Teachings.
Sri Guru Granth Sahib quotes

O Siblings of Destiny, this body and wealth shall not go along with you. The Lord's Name is the pure wealth; through the Guru, God bestows this gift.
Sri Guru Granth Sahib quotes

Those who are attuned to the Love of the Lord, the Architect of Destiny - by serving the Guru, they are known throughout the four ages.
Sri Guru Granth Sahib quotes

Applying oneself to the service of the Guru, the mind is purified, and peace is obtained.
Sri Guru Granth Sahib quotes

True love shall not be broken, if the True Guru is met. Obtaining the wealth of spiritual wisdom, the understanding of the three worlds is acquired.
Sri Guru Granth Sahib quotes

One who does not fear God shall live in fear; without the Guru, there is only pitch darkness.
Sri Guru Granth Sahib quotes

The Diamond of the Guru has pierced the diamond of my mind, which is now dyed in the deep crimson color of the Name.
Sri Guru Granth Sahib quotes

The Guru has cut away my bonds. I shall not have to dance in the wrestling arena of life again. Nanak has searched, and found this opportunity.
Sri Guru Granth Sahib quotes

Abandoning all devices and contrivances, I have sought His Sanctuary. Nanak has fallen at the Feet of the Guru.
Sri Guru Granth Sahib quotes

There is no other as Great as the Guru. I have come and collapsed in the Guru's Sanctuary. In His Kindness, He has united me with God.
Sri Guru Granth Sahib quote

By Guru's Grace, the Lord comes to abide in the mind, and the filth of egotism is dispelled.
Sri Guru Granth Sahib quotes

Servant Nanak is fulfilled, through the Love of the True Guru.
Sri Guru Granth Sahib quotes

You are the father of this animate and inanimate world, and the greatest guru to be worshipped.
Bhagavad Gita

I fall at His Feet to please and appease Him. The True Guru has united me with the Lord, the Primal Being. There is no other as great as He.
Sri Guru Granth Sahib quotes

I am a sacrifice to the True Guru. Meeting Him, the supreme status is obtained.
Sri Guru Granth Sahib quotes

To many in the clergy it may seem heresy to rely so entirely on another person in order to reach God, but in Hinduism the guru is a teacher, preacher, prophet, and the oration of scripture. But what do the scriptures and writings say?

The Lord has declared to the Hindu in His incarnation as Krishna:
"I am in every religion as the thread through a string of pearls. Wherever thou seest extraordinary holiness and extraordinary power raising and purifying humanity, know thou that I am there."
Swami Vivekananda Paper on Hinduism

Desire and the anger due to unfulfilled desires born out of Rajo-guna is all consuming, all sinful and is the biggest foe. -- Gita 3:37

These three desires are not called desires because they do not bind a person.
Desire to see God or desire to love God.
Desire to Realize one's own Self (Atman).
Desire to serve others without selfish motives.
by Swami Ramasukhdasji (Translated From Original Hindi by Swami Radhanandaji)

Abandoning all Dharmas, physically and mentally, surrender to Me alone.
-- Gita 18:66

Shree Krishna repeatedly advises His beloved devotee Uddhava in the Bhagavatam:
"As means to the goal of Self Realization some mention duty, others fame, self-gratification, truth, control of the senses and the mind; yet others mention splendor, gifts, food; and some again sacrifice, austerity, charity, vows or moral rules, universal and particular. The results attained by these means

being the outcome of rituals (desires and expectations) have a beginning and an end (Gita 5:22); produce misery and end in infatuation. They give but transient joy and are attended with grief."

Oh best of the Kurus, I cannot be seen, attained, realized, or experienced by anyone other than yourself in this human world. Neither by the study of Vedas nor by acts of charity, nor by purifactory rituals, and not even by extreme austerities can I be realized.
-- Gita 11:48

This form of Mine which you have seen cannot be realized by mere studies of the Vedas or by austerities, or by acts of charityor by performance of sacrifices.
-- Gita 11:53

O Son of Pandu! He who performs actions for Me who considers Me as the Supreme Goal, who is My devotee and is devoid of attachments; who is without animosity towards all living beings, he alone attains Me (Self, Realization).
-- Gita 11:54, 55

The ultimate message of Lord Krishna in Gitaji is for us to totally surrender to His will alone. (Gita 18: 65, 66.)

Restrain it (the mind) and subjugate it solely to the Self.
-- Gita 6:26

He who, established in oneness, worships Me abiding in all beings.
-- Gita 6:31

He who sees Me everywhere and sees all in Me . . .
-- Gita 6:30

Whose doings are all devoid of design and desire for results
(him the sages will call wise).
-- Gita 4:19

Tell me of the man who lives in wisdom,
Ever aware of the Self, O Krishna;
How does he talk, how sit, how move about?

Sri Krishna:
He lives in wisdom
Who sees himself in all and all in him,
Whose love for the Lord of Love has consumed
Every selfish desire and sense-craving
Tormenting the heart. Not agitated
By grief nor hankering after pleasure,
He lives free from lust and fear and anger
Fettered no more by selfish attachments,
He is not elated by good fortune
Nor depressed by bad. Such is the seer.
Even as a tortoise draws in its limbs
The sage can draw in his senses at will.
An aspirant abstains from sense-pleasures,
But he still craves for them. These cravings all
Disappear when he sees the Lord of Love.
For even of one who treads the path
The stormy senses can sweep off the mind.
But he lives in wisdom who subdues them,
And keeps his mind ever absorbed in me.
When you keep thinking about sense-objects,
Attachment comes. Attachment breeds desire,
The lust of possession which, when thwarted,
Burns to anger. Anger clouds the judgment
And robs you of the power to learn from past mistakes
Lost is the discriminative faculty,
And your life is utter waste.
But when you move amidst the world of sense
From both attachment and aversion freed,

232

There comes the peace in which all sorrows end,
And you live in the wisdom of the Self.
The disunited mind is far from wise;
How can it meditate? How be at peace?
When you know no peace, how can you know joy?
When you let your mind follow the Siren call
Of the senses, they carry away
Your better judgment as a cyclone drives a boat
Off the charted course to its doom.
Use your mighty arms to free the senses
From attachment and aversion alike,
And live in the full wisdom of the Self.
Such a sage awakes to light in the night
Of all creatures. Wherein they are awake
Is the night of ignorance to the sage.

As the rivers flow into the ocean
But cannot make the vast ocean overflow,
So flow the magic streams of the sense-world
Into the sea of peace that is the sage.
He is forever free who has broken out
Of the ego-cage of and mine
To be united with the Lord of Love.
This is the supreme state. Attain thou this
And pass from death to immortality.
- Gita

I am the same to all beings, and my love is ever the same; but
those who worship me with devotion, they are in me and I am
in them.
For if even one who does evil were to worship me with all his
soul, he must be considered righteous, because of his righteous
will.
He will soon become pure and reach everlasting peace. For be
aware, Arjuna, that he who loves me shall not perish.
- Gita 9:29–31

Although I am unmanifest, the unwise think that I am that form of my lower nature which is seen by mortal eyes: they know not my higher nature, imperishable and unsurpassed. -- Gita 7:24

I am the Self, dwelling in the heart of all beings, and the beginning, the middle, and the end of all that lives as well. -- Gita 10:20

Of all knowledge, I am the knowledge of the Soul. Of the many paths of speech, I am the one that leads to Truth. (Gita10:32)

Not by study of the Vedas, nor by an austere life, nor through gift-giving, nor through ritual offerings can I be seen in such a way as you have seen me [i.e., directly within].
Only by undistracted love can men see me, and know me, and enter into me.
He who does my work, who loves me, who sees me as the highest, free from attachment to all things, and with love for all creation, he in truth comes to me.
- Gita 11:53–55

He who offers to me with devotion a leaf, a flower, a fruit, or even a little water, that offering of devotion I accept from him whose self is pure.
Whatever you do, whatever you eat, whatever you offer, whatever you give, whatever austerities you perform, Arjuna, do that as an offering to me.
Thus you will certainly be free from the bonds of karma, from the bondage of good and evil fruits; and with your soul one in the yoga of renunciation you will be liberated and come to me.
- Gita 9:26–28

In every direction I behold your infinite form: innumerable arms, innumerable eyes, innumerable mouths, and

innumerable bellies. Nowhere do I see a beginning or middle or end of you, O Lord of all, whose form is the entire universe! Crowned, armed with a club, bearing a discus, illumining the whole universe, I see you: as blazing fire, as the sun, as immeasurable radiance, beyond seeing or knowing.
- Gita 11:16–17

Love, devotion, unity, liberation, awareness, and enlightenment, whether articulated within holy books of Buddhists, Christians, Jewish, Islam, or the scripture of any major religion that produces a mystical experience all have the same messages, although they may be explained in slightly different ways.

The Secular Mystic

Of all the various types and seats of mysticism, Secular Mysticism may be the most difficult to define, for how can one have a mystical experience and say it is not a "religious" experience? However, like all mystical encounters, it is a spiritual experience which is beyond religion. It is an encounter with the unfathomable complexity and beauty of nature and man. It is a glimpse into man's capacity to feel. It is being a witness to the prime objectives of man: to love and to be loved. This is the call of each and every heart. And it is out of that capacity to feel that is born empathy and compassion. Compassion – the very word speaks of a greater love, for the word itself means "together suffer."

Secular mysticism offers no set concept of a deity, and does not require belief in god at all. Thus, secular mysticism, more than any other form, may rest on how we encounter our fellow man.

According to the German linguist and philosopher, Martin Buber, modern man has come to feel alienated fundamentally because modern society is exclusively an It-world. Existential angst, worries of meaninglessness, and the sense of impending doom that most modern human beings feel at some point in their life (often in the dead of night, when they cannot sleep) are all the result of our strict reliance on experience to the exclusion of encounter.

Buber indicates this one-sided experience is born out of an "I and it" thought process wherein we go through our days relating to our environment and all who are in it as objects. We exchange data with these people/objects as we would with any machine or tool, and in turn others do the same with us.

Buber lays out his argument on how one might escape the trap of isolation and emptiness, beginning with opening ourselves up to encounter and building a society based on relationship that views others, not as tools or units but as people. This, he says, brings us from the "I and it" stage to the stage of "me and you."

In the "You" stage we see others as people, although their opinion and importance may not be viewed as equal to our own, they are now people and not data units or objects. Sadly, the "you and me" position tends to be fleeting and will dissolve once again into the "I and it." This is in part because it is an awareness and not an experience that we are using to change our habit of interaction. We may become aware that we need to change our eating habits and the observation may urge us on to diet or exercise but these changes tend not to last.

Our interaction then, is a constant oscillation between encounter and experience, and it does not wholly fulfill our emptiness. In every human encounter that we undergo, we feel that there could be something deeper, more enduring and more fulfilling. This "more" is an encounter with an absolute and ultimate relation. If we ready ourselves for the encounter it will definitely occur, and the proof that it has taken place will be in the transformation that we undergo. After the absolute encounter we come to see every other being (nature, animals, people) as a "You and me" relationship. And our relationship with the beloved will become "I and Thou." We come to feel affection for everyone and everything, and to have a sense of loving responsibility for the whole course of the world. And as the divine is perceived in us and us in it, we experience this oneness as "I and Thou." This transformation, Buber tells us, is divine revelation. It is salvation. Filled with loving responsibility, given the ability to fully address the world, man is no longer alienated, and does not worry about the meaninglessness of life. He is fulfilled and complete, and will help others to reach this goal as well. He will help to build an ideal society, a real community, which must be made up of people who have also gone through absolute relation, and are therefore willing to say "You" to the entire world. But this can only occur if there is a "Thou" moment. Through our "loving responsibility" we give birth to the ability to see we are equal to and connected with all living things. We truly place ourselves in their position of happiness and suffering. We are open, receptive, and vulnerable.

Drew Leder, PH.d. writes in his book, "Spiritual Passages", "Spiritual love is born of sorrow… For men love one another with spiritual love only when they have suffered the same sorrow together, when through long days they have ploughed the stone ground buried beneath the common yoke of a common grief it is then that they know one another and feel one another in their common anguish, so thus they pity and love one another"

He continues, "Pain makes some people bitter and envious. It makes others sensitive and compassionate. It is the result, not the cause of pain that makes some experiences of pain meaningful and others empty and destructive."

So many people try to sleep through their suffering. Through drinking, drugs, or simply withdrawing from life, they numb and distance themselves from the pain, and therefore gain nothing from the experience. Living brings the opportunity to know bliss and pain and the portions are not distributed equally. On the surface, life is not fair. There is far more pain than joy in the life of many. The majority of times we bring a certain amount of suffering on ourselves by desiring and believing we deserve more than what life offers. It isn't that we should not try to achieve, succeed, and prosper. We simply should not cling and claw and cloud our minds with the worry.

The concept of "Be Here Now" espoused by Ram Doss was straight out of Zen Buddhism's playbook. It is the teaching that encourages us to be totally in the present moment and allow that moment to expand into the eternal now. By being completely aware of "now" and having no part of the mind in the past or future, there is born a mystical experience in everyday life. This is an ancient truth, and truth is discovered over and over in various venues.

In the secular world, the teaching was picked up by Eckhart Tolle when he wrote:
"Wherever you are, be there totally. If you find your here and now intolerable and it makes you unhappy, you have three options: remove yourself from the situation, change it, or accept it totally. If you want to take responsibility for your life, you must choose one of those three options, and you must choose now. Then accept the consequences...
Realize deeply that the present moment is all you ever have. Make the Now the primary focus of your life."

Of the many ways of being in the moment, physical disciplines such as martial arts may be one of the most enigmatic and overlooked of mystical paths. So many disciplines use meditation. Sitting for hours. Bringing the mind back to the present moment each time it wonders and doing so over and over for years until one days it resides for a moment in the eternal present and enlightenment rests on us like a butterfly. Try to attract it and it will elude us. All we can do is wait in the present for the butterfly to alight.

In martial arts the perfect technique is only what is needed. There is nothing added. Every excess motion and thought are whittled away.

Lao Tsu says it like this:
"In the pursuit of knowledge,

Every day something is added.
In the practice of the Tao (Way)
Every day something is dropped."

The meditation of the martial arts is a focused, concentrated act, so mentally concentrated that we abide in every instance of the technique. This results in a powerful insight. It could be an out of body experience where one observes the technique seen from above in seeming slow motion. It could be the perfectly executed technique where the body and mind come into a spiritual balance that feels as if the angels of heaven stand and bow. In either case we come to realize that it is the spirit that drives the body, and they are separate, but must be brought into one accord.

It is when the student suddenly understands the enemy is within us that they realize each technique has always been aimed at themselves. Each punch and each kick was targeted toward the annihilation of the ego, the thing that resists the perfection of technique and self. There is a revelation of separation of body and self. It is the revelation of the unity of all beings on a spiritual level. To be absent from the body is indeed to be present with the Lord – or with that divine sea of humanity. These are the same revelations occurring within mysticism originating from religious paths.

Morihei Ueshiba, the founder of Aikido explains it:
"All people share the same divine origin. There is only one thing that is wrong or useless. That is the stubborn insistence that you are an individual, separate from others. Give thanks and show gratitude. Work for the paradise on this earth. In this way, your true nature will continually unfold."

In the west, and increasingly throughout the world, there is a belief that we must seize control and live life or it will control us. But there is a third option. We can be one with life and allow life to live through us. Life is quite gracious at times and will provide in ways we cannot anticipate, if we listen to what it has to say.

In this way the secular person seeks what is mystical in life without having any roots in religion or forming any set concept of God. That is not to say they are not "religious" in some secular sense, but most describe themselves as spiritual people.

Lloyd Geering, in his book, "Coming Back to Earth: From gods, to God, to Gaia" opens the argument and description of Secular Mysticism. He writes:
"Humans show themselves to be religious whenever and wherever they take the questions of human existence seriously, and then create a common response to whatever they find to be of ultimate value to them. The only truly non-religious person is one who treats human existence as trivial or meaningless, for ultimately the religious phenomenon arises out of human experience as we reflect on the fundamental nature of human existence. With but rare exceptions, people everywhere and at all times have made some kind of response to the demands of human existence. They have tried to make something of life. They have looked for meaning and purpose. They have hoped for some kind of fulfillment. For such reasons humankind has in the past been universally religious, and there is no good reason to suspect that in the future people will cease to be religious. And this is true even though an increasing number have grown dissatisfied with the religious forms of the past, having found them to be irrelevant in the new cultural age we have entered." pp. 151-2

About being a secular mystic, Geering goes on to say:

"To recapture the original meaning of "secular," then, one might propose that its nearest synonym is "this-worldly" and its antonym is "otherworldly." For clearly the modern world has brought a steady increase in our knowledge and understanding of "this-world"--that is, the physical, tangible world. In particular, the discoveries of Galileo, Newton, and Einstein have caused the "other-world" of the heavens to become merged with the "this-world" of our space-time universe. All this has led to a steady decrease in our interest in, or convictions about, any unseen and therefore hypothetical other-world."

....This point was made in a lecture as long ago as 1850 by W.B. Hodgson on "The Secular, the Religious and the Theological," in which he said, "Secular means belonging to the Saeculum or Age, or period of life on this earth, as distinguished from eternity or life to come. It should never have come to mean the opposite of religious. The fact that something may be described as secular does not preclude it from also being religious." pp. 149-150

What happens when religious atheists become secular saints? We gather in community and focus on things that are most important, such as:

An attitude of awe towards this self-evolving universe.
An appreciation of the living ecosphere of this planet.
An appreciation of the capacity of the earth to regenerate itself.
The value to be found in life, in all of its diversity.
An appreciation of the total cultural legacy we have received from our human forbears.
Responsibility for the care of one another.
Responsibility for the kind of planet we pass on to our descendants.

Geering continues:
" Such a spirituality could be called secular mysticism. It is not entirely new, for it is reflected in many insights from the past....In developing a spirituality for today's secular world we must not be primarily concerned with saving our individual

selves, with self-improvement, with introspection, and least of all with any form of navel-gazing. Rather we must be primarily concerned for the welfare of one another, for the future of the human species, and for the health of the planet." pp. 200-1

Like many forward thinkers, Geering was misunderstood. He was tried for heresy in the 1960s by the Presbyterian Church of New Zealand.

Drew Leder sums up the commonalities of the secular mystical experience by listing a few ideas they have in common:
"There is an eternal spirit pervading the universe.
We are a creation of that spirit and we are participating in its essence. The meaning of life is in growing toward and expressing of that divine nature.
Death plays a part in helping us attain that goal by dissolving us from the old and releasing us to grow.
What comes after death depends on what came before and how we have travelled the Spiritual passages."
This seems to mimic the mystics of the Native American community.

Kahlil Gibran gives insight into how the mystic may view the expression of life and death.

Kahlil Gibran –
"Your children are not your children.
They are the sons and daughters of Life's longing for itself.
They come through you but not from you,
And though they are with you yet they belong not to you.

You may give them your love but not your thoughts,
For they have their own thoughts.
You may house their bodies but not their souls,
For their souls dwell in the house of tomorrow,
which you cannot visit, not even in your dreams.

You may strive to be like them,
but seek not to make them like you.
For life goes not backward nor tarries with yesterday.

You are the bows from which your children
as living arrows are sent forth.
The archer sees the mark upon the path of the infinite,
and He bends you with His might
that His arrows may go swift and far.
Let your bending in the archer's hand be for gladness;
For even as He loves the arrow that flies,
so He loves also the bow that is stable.

You would know the secret of death.
But how shall you find it unless you seek it in the heart of life?
The owl whose night-bound eyes are blind unto the day cannot
unveil the mystery of light.
If you would indeed behold the spirit of death, open your heart
wide unto the body of life.
For life and death are one, even as the river and the sea are
one."

We will end this section on Secular Mysticism with a quote by
Khalil Gibran on God.

"In the ancient days, when the first quiver of speech came to
my lips, I ascended the holy mountain and spoke unto God,
saying, 'Master, I am thy slave. Thy hidden will is my law and I
shall obey thee for ever more.'

But God made no answer, and like a mighty tempest passed
away.

And after a thousand years I ascended the holy mountain and
again spoke unto God, saying, 'Creator, I am thy creation. Out
of clay hast thou fashioned me and to thee I owe mine all.'

And God made no answer, but like a thousand swift wings passed away.

And after a thousand years I climbed the holy mountain and spoke unto God again, saying, 'Father, I am thy son. In pity and love thou hast given me birth, and through love and worship I shall inherit thy kingdom.'

And God made no answer, and like the mist that veils the distant hills he passed away.

And after a thousand years I climbed the sacred mountain and again spoke unto God, saying, 'My God, my aim and my fulfillment; I am thy yesterday and thou art my tomorrow. I am thy root in the earth and thou art my flower in the sky, and together we grow before the face of the sun.'

Then God leaned over me, and in my ears whispered words of sweetness, and even as the sea that enfoldeth a brook that runneth down to her, he enfolded me.

And when I descended to the valleys and the plains, God was there also."

Conclusion

There is no place to end this journey or this book. For as many people existing, there will be that many and varied paths to the mystical union. Each soul is different and each will approach the divine in his or her own way. As a mother knows each of her children and interacts with each in the best way, so does the divine touch us, guide us, lead us, and love us.

There are as many pitfalls on the mystical path as there are paths to travel. Rigidity is the personal trap. God will do what is best for us. The divine will engage us as it will. Rules and rigidity limit our ability to dance with the divine.

The most hateful and widespread trap, which will limit not only the strict religious person but also the people they target, is the religious fundamentalism that floods the world today. By declaring a single and unmoving truth a wall is built and "believers" are imprisoned by someone's or some system's interpretation of god and what is wanted and desired by the infinite and divine, which man cannot comprehend. How can a single human, organization, religion, or book sum up and contain the infinite universe and the divine power and truth therein? Such an exclusive approach breeds hate. In many cases we are led to believe that God will send everyone to hell that does not adhere to the doctrines and customs of their particular sect. The problem, of course, is that there are an incredible number of religions and sects that believe this way and each is different.

In the past, the Christian Church put on trial and executed all that did not conform to the faith. They warred with Islam and both sides killed thousands. The Christian Church also killed professing Christians, because they were not the kind of Christians the judge or executioners were.

Today Sunni Muslims are killing Shia Muslims. The animosity between the sects is a disagreement regarding who was supposed to lead the faith after Muhammad's death. Both Sunni and Shia are killing Christians, and in many countries both Islamic and Christian are at war with the Islamic fundamental group, I.S.I.S. The Islamic group, Hamas wishes to destroy Israel.

Think about it – If a religious person decides their way is the only way and everyone outside their religion should be killed and after death they will be judged and sent to hell, the religious person is, by default, sending the non-believer to hell for eternity. This is the height of hatefulness.

Religion, in its basic form, is the enemy of mysticism. If god approaches each person in an individual way, how can one set of rules and one set of rituals deliver individual paths? This is why most mystics may belong to a faith but have transcended it and have seen that god is universal and loves all mankind.

Do you condemn other faiths, sects, religions, or those who say they belong to no religion? Do you actually think god will imprison and incinerate everyone but those who agree with you? You must ask yourself if you believe judgment and hate, decisiveness and haughtiness are part of the mystical path.

Within the core of every religion there are those who reach beyond the walls of churches, synagogues, and mosques. Within religions and sects reside those souls who wish to know all of god, and they rise above the towers of restrictions. In the secular world there are those who reject religious trappings and only want to know the divine. These religious and secular people of love will keep the fires of mysticism burning in their hearts, and it will spread.

If the blood of Christ were precious, God would not spare a single drop from the full purpose of which the sacrifice was intended, and all men would be reconciled to God no matter their color, culture, or religion.
Wanda Adam

Ralph Waldo Emerson stated:
"There is one mind common to all individual men.
Of the works of this mind history is the record. Man is explicable by nothing less than all his history. All the facts of history pre-exist as laws. Each law in turn is made by circumstances predominant. The creation of a thousand forests is in one acorn, and Egypt, Greece, Rome, Gaul, Britain, America, lie folded already in the first man. Epoch after epoch, camp, kingdom, empire, republic, democracy, are merely the application of this manifold spirit to the manifold world".

Vivekananda, an Indian mystic, says it this way:
"Stand upon the spirit, then only can we truly love the world. Take a very, very high stand; knowing our universal nature, we must look with perfect calmness upon all the panorama of the world. This is the secret of spiritual life: to think that I am the spirit and not the body, and that the whole of this universe with all its relations, with all its good and all its evil, is but as a series of paintings - scenes on a canvas - of which I am the witness."

There is not one color in the human pallet. There is not one tone in a song. There is not one type of person. There is not one faith. The mystical experience is found throughout humanity, within every religion that contains truth, and in every person seeking truth deeply. It does not matter which holy book we use or what we have come to name god, or even if we have no holy scripture or concept of god at all, there is a path before us we can choose to walk. The path is not easy, but the destination is ecstasy.

Can any one doubt that if the noblest saint among the Buddhists, the noblest Mahometan, the highest Stoic of Athens, the purest and wisest Christian, - Buddha and Menu in India, Confucius in China, Spinoza in Holland, could somewhere meet and converse, - they would all find themselves of one religion, - would find themselves denounced by their own sects, ...
Emerson's "Essential Principles of Religion" lecture of 1862.

Each nation has its bible more or less pure; none has yet been willing or able in a wise and devout spirit to collate its own with those of other nations, sinking (excluding) the civil-historical and ritual portions, to bring together the grand expressions of the moral sentiment in different ages and races, the rules for the guidance of life, the bursts of piety and of abandonment to the Invisible and Eternal; - a work inevitable sooner or later, and which we hope is to be done by religion and not by literature.
The Dial, III, July 1842, 82; (quoted in R. K. Dhawan, Henry David Thoreau, a Study in Indian Influence, 1985, 27-28)

Yes I am, I am also a Muslim, a Christian, a Buddhist, and a Jew.
Mahatma Gandhi

The great religions are the ships,
Poets the life Boats.
Every sane person I know has jumped overboard.
That is good for business, isn't it
— Daniel Ladinsky

There appears to be discernible agreement between the major world religions as to core Spiritual Truths. One may establish that it is actually possible for a spiritual person to personally self-identify with a particular religion but also deem themselves to be, simultaneously, a follower of other spiritual traditions, because the spirituality they wish to fulfill within their chosen religion can be shown to be similar to the spiritualities upheld by other religious traditions.
Age of the Sage

Truth is truth, and although terms may differ, meaning does not. Comparing writings and attitudes between Christian, Sufi, Hindu, Zen, Islamic, and secular mystics one sees, not so much a pattern as a replication of experience and insight, with differences accounted for due to the lack of usable language for interior spiritual processes.

Where there is truth there is God, for whatever one may envision the deity to be, truth must be at its core. Whether one looks to the universe or to a universal consciousness, one is seeking truth. In all religions, faiths, and spiritual practices, the mystics within these manifold systems reach, attain, and articulate the same truth. We are spirit. We are one. The divine awaits us. The road is love. The destination is freedom.

Truth is always with us, in us, around us, but we are like fish, swimming in the pure water, dying of thirst.

Joseph Lumpkin

BIBLIOGRAPHY

The Bible. King James Version, unless otherwise noted.

Burghardt, Walter J., S.J. The Image of God in Man according to Cyril of Alexandria. Washington: Catholic University of America Press, 1957.

Cyril of Alexandria. Commentary on the Gospel of St. Luke. Trans. Robert Payne Smith. United States: Studion Publishers, 1983.

Cyril of Alexandria. Cyril of Alexandria: Select Letters. Trans. Lionel R. Wickham. Oxford: Oxford University Press, 1983.

Cyril of Alexandria. On the Unity of Christ. Trans. John Anthony McGuckin. Crestwood, NY: St. Vladimir's Seminary Press, 1995.

The sayings of the Desert Fathers : the alphabetical collection. Trans. Benedicta Ward, SLG. Kalamazoo, Michigan: Cistercian Publications Inc., 1984, 1975.

Gregory of Nazianzus. Orations. Trans. under the editorial supervision of Philip Schaff and Henry Wace.

International Consultation on English Texts (ICET) and the English Language Liturgical Consultation (ELLC)

John Climacus. The Ladder of Divine Ascent. Trans. Colm Luibheid and Norman Russell. Mahwah, New Jersey: Paulist Press, 1982.

The Lenten Triodion, liturgical prayers recited by the Eastern Orthodox Church during the season of Lent. The nten Triodion. Trans. The Community of the Holy Myrrbearers. The Lenten

Triodion. Trans. Mother Mary and Archimandrite Kallistos Ware. London: Faber and Faber, 1977.

St. Nikodimos of the Holy Mountain and St. Makarios of Corinth. The Philokalia, The Complete Text. Trans. G.E.H. Palmer; Philip Sherrard; and Kallistos Ware. London: Faber and Faber Limited, (Vol. 1) 1979, (Vol. 2) 1981

Symeon the New Theologian. Symeon the New Theologian: The Discourses. Trans. C.J. de Catanzaro. Ramsey, N.J.: Paulist Press, 1980. Symeon the New Theologian. On the Mystical Life: The Ethical Discourses. Trans. Alexander Golitzin. Crestwood, NY: St. Vladimir's Seminary Press, 1996.

Angela of Foligno. Angela of Foligno: Complete Works. Mahwah, New Jersey: Paulist Press, 1993.

Anonymous. The Cloud of Unknowing and Other Works. Trans. Clifton Wolters. New York: Penguin Books USA, Inc., 1961, 1978.

Catherine of Siena. Catherine of Siena: The Dialogue.Trans. Suzanne Noffke, O.P. Mahwah, New Jersey: Paulist Press, 1980.

St. John of the Cross, a Spanish Mystic, who lived from 1542 to 1591. John of the Cross. Ascent of Mount Carmel. Trans. E. Allison Peers.

Julian of Norwich, an English mystic who lived from 1342 to 1413. Julian of Norwich. Revelations of Divine Love. Ed. Grace Warrack

Brother Lawrence of the Resurrection. The Practice of the Presence of God. Mount Vernon, NY: Peter Pauper Press, Inc., 1963.

Bonaventure by Ewert Cousins Mahwah, New Jersey: Paulist Press, 1978

Thomas Merton. Thoughts in solitude. Boston: Shambhala Publications, Inc., 1956, 1958.

Nicholas of Cusa. Nicholas of Cusa: Selected Spiritual Writings. Trans. Hugh Lawrence Bond. Mahwah, New Jersey: Paulist Press, 1997.

Teresa of Avila. Interior Castle. Trans. E. Allison Peers. New York: Bantam Doubleday Dell Publishing Group, Inc., 1990.

Teachings of the Christian Mystics by Andrew Harvey; Shambala Boston and London

Thomas à Kempis. The Imitation of Christ. Trans. Richard Whitford, moderenized by Harold C. Gardiner. New York: Doubleday, 1955.

Jacob Boehme. The Supersensual Life. Trans. William Law.

A. W. Tozer. The Pursuit of God. Wheaton, Ill.: Tyndale House, 1982.

Meister Eckhart. Meister Eckhart: Selected Writings. Trans. Oliver Davies. New York: Penguin Books USA, Inc., 1994.

Jeanne-Marie Bouvier de la Motte-Guyon. Autobiography of Madame Guyon.

Marguerite Porete. Marguerite Porete: The Mirror of Simple Souls. Trans. Ellen L. Babinsky. Mahwah, New Jersey: Paulist Press, 1993.

Mysticism in World Religions by Deb Platt

Wikipedia, the free encyclopedia.

W.R. Lumpkin A Southern Baptist pastor of more than 25 years.

Sacred-Text (collections on DVD)

The writings of Om Shanti Guru Swami G

Lloyd Geering: A Religious Atheist and a Secular Mystic: review written Thursday, October 22, 2009

The Dhammapada, A Collection of Verses, Being One of the Canonical Books of the Buddhists, Translated from Pali by F. Max Muller

Feasting at Wisdom's Table, Published by Fifth Estate, by Joseph Lumpkin

Look for other fine books by Joseph Lumpkin.

www.fifthestatebooks.com
www.fifthestatebooks.com

Printed in Great Britain
by Amazon